THE
SPIAGGIA COOKBOOK

the spiaggia cookbook

ELEGANZA ITALIANA IN CUCINA

By Tony Mantuano and Cathy Mantuano

Foreword by Larry Levy and Photographs by Jeff Kauck

CHRONICLE BOOKS

SAN FRANCISCO

Library of Congress Cataloging-in-Publication Data:

Mantuano, Tony, 1954–

The Spiaggia cookbook : eleganza italiana in cucina / by Tony Mantuano and Cathy Mantuano; foreword by Larry Levy; photographs by Jeff Kauck.

p. cm.

ISBN 0-8118-4511-7

1. Cookery, Italian. 2. Spiaggia (Restaurant) I. Mantuano, Cathy, 1958– II. Title.

TX723.M323 2004

641.5945–dc22

2004002641

Manufactured in China

Food stylist: Will Smith

Levy Restaurants Creative Director: Kirsten Mentley

Book Designer: Lisa Billard Design, NY

Typeset in Chasline, News 701 BT, and Zurich BT

Aceto Balsamico di Modena Villa Manodori® is a registered trademark of Massimo Bottura, Aceto Balsamico Giovanna Pavarotti di Modena Italia® is a registered trademark of Acetaia Giovanna Pavarotti Modena S.R.L., Acquerello® is a registered trademark of Rondolino P.S.C.A. A.r.l., Agrumato® is a registered trademark of Mediterranea s.r.l., Alfonso's® is a registered trademark of Alfonso's Food Products Ltd., Bella di Cerignola® is a registered trademark of Bioconserve S.R.L., Illy® is a registered trademark of illycaffè S.p.A., Kahlúa® is a registered trademark of The Kahlúa Company, Moscato Allegro® is a registered trademark of Martin & Weyrich Winery LLC, Moretti® is a registered trademark of Molini Riuniti S.p.A., Nueske® is a registered trademark of Nueske's Hillcrest Farm, Parmigiano-Reggiano is a registered trademark of Consorzio del Formaggio Parmigiano-Reggiano Consortium Italy, Prosciutto di San Daniele SD® is a registered trademark of Consorzio Del Prosciutto di San Daniele, Sid Wainer & Son HACCP® is a registered trademark of Friendly Fruit, Inc., Valrhona® is a registered trademark of Valrhona S.A.

Distributed in Canada by Raincoast Books

9050 Shaughnessy Street

Vancouver, BC V6P 6E5

10 9 8 7 6 5 4 3 2

Chronicle Books LLC

85 Second Street

San Francisco, California 94105

www.chroniclebooks.com

Find out more about Spiaggia at www.spiaggiarestaurant.com

SPIAGGIA

table of contents

○○ mozzarella di bufala con peperoni arrostiti, carciofi, olive cerignola e pesto Fresh Mozzarella Cheese with Roasted Peppers, Artichokes, Cerignola Olives, and Ligurian Pesto 75

○○ cardi con fonduta Cardoons with Fontina Cheese Sauce 76

○○ scampi alla griglia all'olio extra virgine di oliva, limone e prezzemolo Billy's Langoustinos 79

I PRIMI pasta, risotto, and soup 80

Tips for Making Pasta 82, Tips for Making Risotto 82, Making Pasta Using the Tools of Antiquity 84

○○ corzetti con polpa di granchio, pancetta, rucola e pomodorini
Hand-Stamped Pasta Disks with Crab, Pancetta, Arugula, and Cherry Tomatoes 86

○○ spaghetti alla chitarra con gamberoni rossi e zucchine
"Guitar String" Pasta with Red Shrimp and Baby Zucchini 89

○○ bigoli alle castagne in salsa di porcini Handmade Pasta Tubes with Porcini Mushroom Sauce 90

○○ gnocchi di patate con coniglio brasato Potato Pasta Dumplings with Braised Rabbit 93

○○ tagliatelle ai tartufi bianchi Homemade Pasta Ribbons with White Truffles 96

○○ fagottini all'aragosta con dragoncello
"Hobo Sack" Pasta with Lobster and Lobster Tarragon Sauce 99

○○ agnolotti di vitello con polline di finocchio
Veal-Filled Crescent Ravioli with Crispy Veal Breast and Fennel Pollen 101

○○ ravioletti di crescenza con salsa di Parmigiano-Reggiano e burro al tartufo
Crescenza Ravioli with Parmigiano-Reggiano and Truffle Butter Sauce 104

○○ cappellacci di zucca con salvia Pasta Hats with Pumpkin and Sage 107

○○ risotto con pancetta, peperoni e succo d'uva
Risotto with Melrose Peppers, Braised Pork Belly, and Verjus 109

○○ zuppa gran faro Tuscan Bean and Spelt Soup 112

I SECONDI main courses

foreword: *IL MIO SOGNO REALIZZATO* (MY DREAM COME TRUE)

I was enjoying a delicious plate of pasta with sea dates, the most exotic of shellfish, when the inspiration for Spiaggia came to me. My Italian friend Vando D'Angiolo was treating me to a spectacular lunch at Bistrot Ristorante, located right on the sparkling Mediterranean beach in Forti dei Marmi. I was there to buy granite and marble from Vando for a one-million-square-foot mixed-use building I was planning to build on the famed corner of Oak Street and Michigan Avenue in Chicago. As lunch progressed, I fantasized about having a jewel box of an Italian restaurant as the centerpiece of this fabulous new building. The restaurant space would overlook Chicago's Oak Street Beach on the shores of Lake Michigan at the northernmost point of the Magnificent Mile.

Italians from Milan, Rome, and Florence make the time-honored *vacanza* pilgrimage with their families to Forti dei Marmi each August. They relax on the beautiful beaches and swarm the seaside restaurants and cafés to savor the delicious cooking of this charming city on the Tuscan coast. As I observed these rituals—this way of life—and the joy of the Italian people, I wanted to bring it all back home with me. I have always been passionate about all things Italian: the food, the wines, the cars, the clothes, the cities, the people and their culture. I am as passionate about my hometown of Chicago as I am about Italy, and I feel fortunate to have built my business and settled my family here.

Spiaggia means "beach" in Italian, and when we picked the name it all started to come together. I envisioned delicious, authentic Italian meals with fantastic regional Italian wines being served to Chicago's leading locals and visitors in a tiered setting where every guest could view Chicago's *spiaggia*. I pictured beautiful custom *rosso levanto* marble columns from Forte dei Marmi adorning the dining room. I imagined romantics proposing marriage, families celebrating special occasions, and investment bankers toasting their biggest deals. That's how Spiaggia was conceived.

So the seed was planted. As I began construction at the One Magnificent Mile address in 1980, I started my search for a truly great chef who could share my vision and be the creative genius to bring it to life. One of our employees, Cathy Roeske, while working with my mother, Eadie, at the Chestnut Street Grill (then the best of the four Levy Restaurants), spoke often of the talents of her fantastic fiancé, Tony Mantuano, who was, according to her, an outstanding Italian chef.

I decided to give Tony's food a try and invited him to cook for my wife, Carol, and some of our friends at a dinner party in our home. On that memorable night, I remember the late Gene Siskel giving the meal "two thumbs up," along with my brother Mark and many of our other good friends. We all knew instantly that I had found the maestro who would orchestrate the vision that was to become Spiaggia. The first step was clear to me: I sent Tony and Cathy, now his wife, off to Italy for a year. They were able to immerse themselves in the culture of Italy, working in the very best restaurants throughout the country, and they carried that experience back to Spiaggia.

I have been an entrepreneur for over thirty-five years, principally as a restaurateur and real estate developer on a large scale. Entrepreneurs are dreamers first. Whenever I am asked which is my favorite "dream become reality," I always answer with Spiaggia: It is, I feel, my most perfect vision and execution. I am certain that my love for Italian culture helped me in making my dream of Spiaggia come true.

During the last twenty years, Spiaggia has wined and dined the famous, the infamous, trendy "foodies," and some of the most discerning palates in the world. We have hosted with much success and pride Sir Elton John, the late Princess Diana, Sir Mick Jagger, Julia Roberts, Billy Joel, Harrison Ford, Sting, Tom Cruise, President Clinton, Paul Newman, Steven Spielberg, and Sir Paul McCartney. (Tony created a special five-course vegetarian menu per Sir Paul's request that magical evening; the meal was such a hit, the menu has become a permanent seasonal feature, delighting vegetarians and meat eaters alike.) Spiaggia is as much for family and loved ones sharing great food as for luminaries, or for special events. Carol and I have had too many memorable dinners at Spiaggia to count, with our four sons, their wives, our grandchildren, my mother, Eadie, and our dearest friends.

Many of the great chefs of America and Europe have visited Spiaggia, including Alice Waters, Wolfgang Puck, Charlie Trotter, Rick Bayless, Gordon Ramsay, David Bouley,

Paul Bocuse, Joël Robuchon, Ferran Adrìa, Mark Miller, Daniel Boulud, Jean Banchet, Rocco DiSpirito, and many others. Our grandson Riley may turn out to be a great American chef, although it's a little early to tell at six years old. (I will never forget Riley's excitement the night we brought him to Spiaggia to meet his idol, Emeril Lagasse.) Many important winemakers from Italy have dined at Spiaggia, among them Angelo Gaja, Maurizio Zanella, Marchesi de' Frescobaldi, Piero Antinori, Silvio Jermann, Paolo Marzotto, and Francesca Planeta, as well as Randall Grahm and innumerable other fine Italian varietal producers here in America.

Like a proud father, I can't resist singing the praises of Spiaggia, but my raves are confirmed by the culinary industry. Spiaggia has won virtually every culinary award, including the Ivy Award, the Oscar of the restaurant industry. The *Chicago Tribune* and *Chicago Magazine* rate Spiaggia four stars. Vando D'Angiolo, to me the quintessential Italian, says that Spiaggia would be one of the three best restaurants in Italy. Chef Tony Mantuano has developed into a major star on the world's food stage. His innate brilliance and creativity inspire his talented staff, the guests he serves each day, and me. His sommelier counterpart, Henry Bishop III, has been acknowledged as one of the foremost experts in America on Italian wines. Cathy Mantuano played an instrumental role on Spiaggia's management team and now focuses her talents on food writing and wine consulting.

I hope you enjoy this cookbook as much as I have enjoyed the wonderful meals and my experiences at Spiaggia. As you make these recipes, cook with joy and love, for that is how they were created. I urge you to pair these recipes with the great wines of Italy, which have finally won the international respect and admiration they have so long deserved. And come—or come back—to visit all of us at Spiaggia soon!

—Larry Levy
Founder and chairman of Levy Restaurants, owner of Spiaggia

WELCOME TO spiaggia

IN THE EARLY 1980s, THE INCREASING POPULARITY FOR UPSCALE ITALIAN FOOD
WAS CONSIDERED TO BE A YUPPIE INFATUATION. ESTABLISHED *RISTORANTI*,
DESPITE THEIR ELEGANT DÉCOR AND TUXEDOED STAFF, WERE OFTEN CONSIDERED
FRENCH INSPIRED. OTHER ITALIAN RESTAURANTS WERE EITHER ITALIAN AMERICAN
ESTABLISHMENTS WHERE RED SAUCE WAS KING, OR PIZZA PALACES, WHOSE ONLY
RELATIONSHIP TO AUTHENTIC ITALIAN PIZZA WAS THE WORD ITSELF. MORE
AMERICANS WERE NOW TRAVELING TO ITALY, AND UPON THEIR RETURN, WANTED
THE ITALIAN CUISINE THEY HAD TASTED THERE. THE TIME WAS RIPE FOR A NEW
CLASS OF ITALIAN RESTAURANT: RESTAURANTS THAT COULD DIRECTLY IMPORT
MODERN CUISINE, REGIONAL WINE, AND GENUINE CULTURE HOME TO THE
STATES. AT THAT TIME, CONTEMPORARY ITALIAN CUISINE WAS VIRTUALLY NONEX-
ISTENT IN AMERICA.

The enterprise that would grow to become the restaurant and real estate empire
of the Levy Organization was founded by Larry Levy and his brother, Mark, in 1976.
D. B. Kaplan's Delicatessen was their very first restaurant. With a menu based on
many of their mother's recipes, the small deli on the seventh floor of Chicago's famed
Water Tower Place was a hit. The real estate division of the company also began
to flourish, and by the early 1980s the company owned and operated more than a dozen
restaurants in the Chicago area. After signing several prestigious restaurant develop-
ment deals, the company catapulted into a new league in the business world.

In 1980, the Levy Organization began construction of the $100 million One Magnificent
Mile building located on the prime corner of Michigan Avenue and Oak Street. The high-
rise would be built facing Lake Michigan and take advantage of the view of Oak Street
Beach. Oak Street was then, and still is, Chicago's high-fashion street. All the big
names—Prada, Frette, Tods, Barneys, Jil Sanders, Ultimo—are there. Oak Street and
Michigan Avenue form the northernmost corner of the Magnificent Mile. To the south,
Michigan Avenue is lined with fine hotels and shops, while the John Hancock building
towers over it all. North of Oak and Michigan are the prestigious neighborhoods of
the Gold Coast and Lincoln Park. Looking out to Oak Street Beach, wrapped in pink
granite with marble columns and tiered floors, Spiaggia—named, simply enough, for
the word "beach" in Italian—was launched.

As part of his vision of authenticity for Spiaggia, in 1983, Larry Levy sent us to live in Italy and study cooking with its native chefs. In Milan we met with Eugenio Medagliani, administrative president of the Italian National Association of Professional Chefs. Medagliani connected restaurateurs around the world with Italian chefs, and had arranged for us to work around the country in distinguished family-owned restaurants. These restaurants formed a group named Linea Italia in Cucina, known for its philosophy of cooking traditional regional food in a modern, updated, and professional fashion. After a few months, Medagliani made mention of the fact that we were the first Americans he had ever encountered working and studying in Italian restaurants with the sole purpose of returning to the States to create an authentic Italian dining experience, serving up food both true to its origins and on the forefront of modern Italian cuisine.

We began our work at Al Bersagliere, a restaurant and small inn near the town of Mantova. The restaurant was owned by two brothers named Ferrari and run by their sons, Massimo in the kitchen and Roberto in the dining room. All the family members had jobs: during service, mothers, fathers, sisters, brothers, and wives had their stations in the kitchen; the other brothers and husbands attended to the guests and served the wine. The menu comprised regional specialties, yet was influenced by French technique and presentation. Just outside the windows of the dining room, the peaceful Mincio River flowed by, creating the feeling that you'd just escaped to the countryside. Celebrations of all kinds took place in Al Bersagliere's elegant party room downstairs, which opened onto a rose-filled courtyard near the river's edge. The Ferrari family strived for perfection. The tuxedo-clad waiters actually wore white gloves during service!

After Mantova, we traveled to a small, rural farming town one hour south of Milan to study at Dal Pescatore, a restaurant with only forty seats. Operated by Antonio and Nadia Santini, Dal Pescatore gave its customers very personalized food and service. Nadia directed the kitchen and, although six months pregnant with their second child at the time, never missed a day at the stove. Antonio guided guests through the menu, selected wines to match, and took care of all the front of the house details. Antonio's parents, who also lived and farmed on the property, raised chickens and harvested lake fish, maintained a large herb and vegetable garden, and cooked with Nadia in the kitchen.

Though it was originally a small roadhouse for the local farmers and for travelers passing through, Nadia and Antonio fashioned Dal Pescatore into perhaps the most elegant dining room in all of Italy. The menu offered local specialties and other Lombardian dishes, refined and fashionably served. Clientele from Milan regularly drove to this culinary oasis for lunch or dinner. The unique dining experience the Santinis created at Dal Pescatore made a great impression on us, and we wanted to create a similar sophistication and elegance for Spiaggia, combining tradition, comfort, and quality.

Moving on to Tuscany, Cathy and I continued our training at the Brunicardi family's bustling trattoria La Mora, near the town of Lucca. Sauro Brunicardi graciously ran the dining room while his wife and mother assisted in the kitchen. Unlike the other family-run restaurants we had seen, La Mora employed a chef and a full-time kitchen staff. From the surrounding hills, farmers would bring goat's and sheep's milk cheeses, whole baby lamb, giant porcini mushrooms, and all kinds of aromatics to the kitchen door. We were envious; this way of getting products for the day's menu was infinitely better than the systems back home. La Mora used a variety of olive oils from all over Tuscany for their bountiful *cucina dell'introterra* (inland cuisine).

Another Tuscan restaurant that influenced the culinary vision for Spiaggia was Da Romano, a small but busy place in the seaside town of Viareggio. Located just a few blocks from the sea, Da Romano was known for the freshest local seafood on the coast. Romano Franceschini himself provided the service and his wife, Franca, did the cooking. No one ever saw a menu at Da Romano; with Romano's guidance, diners would make meals of the many small plates Franca had created for that day with her shellfish and seafood artistry. Romano's cellar consisted of a wide selection of Tuscan wines. Their own vineyard produced the excellent house wines.

Franco Colombani, the president of Linea Italia in Cucina, housed his restaurant, Al Sole, in a fifteenth-century villa just south of Milan. Surrounded by low white walls, the villa hid guest rooms, an outdoor kitchen, and a large courtyard. The restaurant kitchen was cozy and charming. Meat entrées were roasted in the large fireplace that divided the kitchen from the main dining room. Near the fireplace sat a long table with chairs for dining that was lovingly called *la tavola d'amici* (the table of friends). This was the place where regulars and locals would eat, families would gather, and at times strangers became friends. It was the way people ate in that very restaurant back in 1463, Colombani surmised. He liked tradition and was fascinated with old recipes culled from his substantial collection of antique cookbooks. Colombani had fun with the old recipes. When a contest in Milan was held to see who could create the best new dish of the trendy *nuova cucina* movement (the Italian version of French *nouvelle cuisine*), Colombani gave a friend one of his seventeenth-century recipes to prepare. Presented elegantly, appearing quite modern, and satisfying contemporary tastes, the dish won the contest. Colombani helped us further understand how to look for inspiration from tradition.

You don't have to be a chef to recognize how Italian cuisine in America has changed over the past twenty years. Perhaps the most important aspect of the change is that Americans now know about and want authentic regional Italian food. This in turn has driven the demand for and availability of genuine Italian foodstuffs. There are more imported Italian products in today's marketplace than ever before. The at-home cook can go to almost any major supermarket or shop on-line for ingredients. All over the country, there are increased numbers of better Italian-inspired dining options, from the take-out sections in grocery stores to formal Italian *ristoranti*. The Italian food phenomenon has been growing, with no apparent sign of reaching its peak.

In this book, you'll find traditional regional Italian recipes that were written with modern eating habits in mind. We also recommend using the best-quality ingredients and the freshest seasonal produce when cooking at home, as we do in Spiaggia's kitchens. In writing this cookbook, we invite you to share the strategies that have made Spiaggia unique.

As we tell all our Spiaggia stories, our goal is to bring you the flavors of real Italian cuisine, a slice of food history, and a sip of wine culture.

learning to enjoy food as italians do:
SEASON BY SEASON

THE FIRST AND MOST IMPORTANT RULE WE LEARNED IN ITALY WAS THAT PROD-
UCT QUALITY AND FRESHNESS WROTE THE MENU OF THE DAY. CHEFS ACHIEVED
THAT OPTIMAL QUALITY AND FRESHNESS BY CHOOSING DISHES WITH RESPECT
FOR THE SEASON. IN THE AMERICAN CULINARY ARENA AT THAT TIME, THE SEASONS
DIDN'T SEEM TO PLAY MUCH OF A ROLE—AMERICANS DINED AT A PARTICULAR
TYPE OF RESTAURANT FOR A PARTICULAR TYPE OF MEAL, AND RESTAURANTS
SOUGHT TO SATISFY THOSE DEMANDS YEAR-ROUND.

Shopping every day for ingredients was essential to the principle of freshness, and those excursions were half the fun for us in Italy. Every street had shops displaying beautiful fresh produce. Inside white-tiled seafood markets, merchants presented a wide variety of fish, many whole or cut into fillets with the skin still on. Small red mullet and the tiniest of clams were unlike any seafood we had ever seen! Some shops only sold pork products; all kinds of salamis and prosciutti hung from the ceilings. The selection of cheeses made from sheep's milk and goat's milk alone was astounding. Even the bars made sandwiches with chewy, crusty bread. The sights and smells were intoxicating.

In Italy, there is a close connection to where food comes from, and a truly personal effort is made to ensure quality, freshness, and flavor. Italian cuisine is based on finding the best ingredients and preparing them simply:

○○ At Dal Pescatore, the day started with going to the garden and picking herbs and vegetables for the lunch service. Eggs were collected from the chickens, and perhaps a chicken was taken for broth. Freshwater fish were caught "to order" from the small pond in the tranquil backyard that doubled as the view from the dining room windows.

○○ At Al Bersagliere, the family raised their own pigs to make the local cured-meat delicacy called *culatello*, known as the heart of the prosciutto. In the afternoon, between lunch and dinner, the women of Al Bersagliere would make their fresh egg pasta using a skinny rolling pin that was as long as a baseball bat. They rolled the pasta so thin it became translucent. Al Bersagliere was known for *tortelli di zucca*, little pasta pockets stuffed with fresh pumpkin, cookie crumbs, and Parmigiano-Reggiano cheese, served with melted butter and sage. A local specialty of note from a recipe dating to the late sixteenth century, this sweet-savory dish is a revelation, and just one of the many treasures from Italy that we've adapted for this book.

○○ Da Romano served only the freshest fish and shellfish. They were caught that morning just down the street from the restaurant, and the quality and variety were incredible.

○○ La Mora specialized in beef, lamb, and game dishes. They served a wonderful pasta sauce made from wild marjoram that grew in the hills to the north. The Serchio River, which ran past La Mora's back door, provided delicate, small fish that were often caught and quickly fried as an appetizer.

Italy was not unified as a country until the nineteenth century. In fact, even today, many Italians identify themselves by their regional birthplace rather than their country. The regional differences in Italy are powerful and distinct. A recipe for gnocchi from Piedmont can be substantially different than a recipe for gnocchi from Lazio, and gnocchi from Sardinia don't seem like gnocchi at all. These regional differences give Italian cuisine its character and appeal.

We learned a lot traveling in Italy and still do every time we return. Oddly, the more we learned, the more we realized our families had been showing us many of the same truths since childhood. We both grew up in big Italian families, where food and wine played a major role in our lives. Every day on the way home from school, Tony would stop at the Mantuano Food Shop to see his grandparents. His grandfather was the butcher, and his grandmother ran the cash register and just about everything else. The store was located in the old Italian neighborhood in the heart of Kenosha, Wisconsin. Tony loved the way the store smelled of cheese, herbs, salamis, and olives. His grandparents knew all their customers by name and would take extra time to ask about their families and about mutual friends. His grandfather kept the favored cuts of meat for the regulars. His grandparents always seemed to know exactly what people wanted.

Each spring, Tony's grandparents planted a massive vegetable garden. By late summer, the tomato plants were over five feet tall. The peppers, zucchini, eggplants, and beans thrived. His grandparents took pride in their garden. After dinner, when the older Italian couples in the neighborhood took their evening stroll, passing by the garden, his grandfather would invite them in to get a closer look. They talked about gardening tips, weather, and favorite recipes. By the end of the evening, his grandparents would give their *paesani* a few tomatoes or zucchini to take home with them. At harvesttime, his grandfather would take the seeds from the biggest, strongest plants to use for next year's planting.

Cathy's grandparents came from Molise, in central Italy. She has early memories of the small shed in the backyard where her grandfather's homemade pressings of Muscat and Zinfandel grapes were made into wine. "Pa's wine" (as Cathy's mother called it) was considered more than just a beverage to serve with a meal; he was proud of his wine, and being offered a glass was a true extension of friendship, an invitation to become acquainted with his culture.

Both of our grandmothers were excellent cooks. Recipes passed down from their mothers had been passed down from their mothers before them. Nothing was written down; cooking was a matter of circumstance and intuition. For example, if the weather was a little humid, a recipe would have to be modified. Grandma Mantuano couldn't tell us exactly how a recipe needed to be changed; it just had to feel right or taste right. To learn from our grandmothers, we had to watch carefully. Sometimes we would catch Grandma Mantuano adding an ingredient that she had never, at least to us, included before. We would accuse her of keeping secrets, but she would just laugh and wave a hand, saying it was something she had always done. She liked the fact that Tony had become a chef. "We are alike," she once told him. Grandmothers and chefs didn't need recipes, she said; "We cook from the heart."

The course of Italian cuisine in America has been one of popularity following tradition. Though it was based originally on "mama's cooking" and the specialties of Italy's southern regions, Americans have come to embrace the diverse regional foods of Italy. Over the last two decades, Spiaggia has been proud to bring real Italian cuisine and imported Italian products to the dining public. We are also proud to have played a big part in the countrywide movement advocating an appreciation for using the freshest, seasonal ingredients of the highest quality available for any meal.

Although we have highlighted our memories of living and cooking in Italy throughout this book, it is the philosophy of the meal in Italy that is fundamental to our ongoing vision at Spiaggia. Italians believe that if they give special attention to choosing foods that are fresh, natural, and lovingly prepared, the foods will in turn nurture and replenish both body and soul. While eating is a matter of survival, sharing a meal is a ritual that is essential to our relationships, connecting the lives of family and friends. It is a way of celebrating each new day.

The Spiaggia Cookbook is not just a souvenir of a world-class restaurant, but a resource for those who love the discoveries that are made when adventuring with food and wine. It is a book for those who enjoy cooking, eating, and drinking. And we hope it helps you enjoy food as Italians do: season by season.

—Tony Mantuano, chef and partner of Spiaggia, and
  Cathy Mantuano, food and wine writer

fundamentals OF THE SPIAGGIA KITCHEN

Basic Principles

In writing this book, we have tried to re-create as closely as possible the dishes Spiaggia serves, while making the recipes accessible to the home cook. Following some of the core principles operating at Spiaggia will help you achieve optimum success when preparing these recipes in your kitchen.

oo Use only the freshest ingredients; this cannot be emphasized enough. Your taste buds will be rewarded for the extra effort you make in seeking out the best-possible ingredients.

oo Cook with the seasons, planning menus and choosing the freshest products according to the time of year at hand.

oo Use sea salt (see below), freshly ground pepper, and fresh herbs whenever possible.

oo Always taste for seasoning in sauces and dressings before serving.

oo Assume medium size bowls for mixing ingredients, unless otherwise specified.

Basic Ingredients

butter These recipes specify unsalted butter. When reducing sauces and seasoning to taste at different stages, salted butter can make a dish, well, too salty. You don't need to use imported butter; butter from a local dairy is most likely fresher, and you can feel good about supporting your local farmer.

caul The thin membrane that lines the abdominal cavity of pigs and sheep. We use pork caul. Caul is wrapped around meats or fish and melts away during cooking. Using caul keeps meat juicy; it is also used to keep fresh herbs on the meat while cooking. Caul is found in the meat case of well-stocked supermarkets or can be ordered from your local butcher. Caul fat can be stored frozen. Cut caul sheets into usable squares and layer between waxed paper. Wrap in plastic and freeze for up to 1 month.

caviar At Spiaggia we like to use caviar as a condiment to enhance a dish. Caviar adds an extra element of flavor and freshness to oysters, lobster, crabmeat, and raw fish. When it comes to caviar, osetra is our favorite. Osetra is brownish gray in color and possesses a subtle nutty flavor. Only a small amount of caviar per serving is needed to enrich a dish dramatically. Lobster roe is not nearly as expensive as osetra, and we use it for color as well as texture. Caviar can be purchased at your local seafood store.

eggs When it comes to cooking with eggs, freshness is critical. All of Spiaggia's recipes assume the use of large eggs. You may notice that some recipes include raw eggs. It is recommended not to serve dishes containing raw eggs to very young children, people with compromised immune systems, pregnant women, or the elderly.

flour Spiaggia uses a variety of flours. Semolina, or durum wheat flour, is what we use to make all our pasta. For the lightest, most tender pasta, use semolina labeled 00 Farina di Grano Tenero (the 00 refers to its soft, finely ground texture). Italians use this flour for pasta; more and more widely available in U.S. stores, type 00 is the best semolina flour you can buy.

foie gras Foie gras, a special delicacy, is the liver of a goose or duck that has been fed a special diet. Foie gras is graded in three levels. Grade A is the top, and is used in recipes that call for sautéing. B grade is recommended for terrines, and grade C has a texture best used for pâté. Foie gras is sold in lobes, and should be trimmed of visible green bile fat and soaked, refrigerated, in milk overnight to draw out any impurities. After soaking, pat the liver dry and carefully remove any veins with a toothpick. Usually eaten early in the meal but also appearing as a filling in main courses, foie gras is richly flavored and has a buttery, smooth texture.

herbs, fresh Another signature of Italian cuisine, fresh herbs are essential in the Spiaggia kitchen. We use fresh herbs whenever possible, although dried herbs will do for some purposes. Basil, rosemary, thyme, sage, mint, and flat-leaf (Italian) parsley are just a few of the herbs Italians have been cooking with for centuries that are easy to grow; most of them can be found in well-stocked supermarkets year-round.

olive oil The recipes call for extra-virgin olive oil, which is the oil that comes from the first cold pressing of the olives. To be called extra-virgin, the oil must have less than 1 percent acidity. As a general rule, the lower the acidity, the better. Some olive oils are fruity, while others are pungent and peppery; these differences in flavor come from the type of olive used and where the olives are grown.

Every year at Spiaggia, we taste olive oils from all over Italy to select the one we choose as our own. That oil is our mainstay, but we also use other oils to enhance dishes. Olive oils from Tuscany are usually made from a blend of olive varieties. We recommend looking for olive oils produced by wineries. Wineries like Tenuta di Cappezana or Monte Vertine produce high-quality estate oils that are exquisite as a condiment. Ligurian olive oils made from Taggiasca olives are prized for their balance of fruity and fresh flavors. Sicilian olive oils like Ravida or Planeta are herbaceous and are excellent with salads and over grilled fish. Citrus-infused olive oils from southern Italy are refreshing options with shellfish. Almost every region in Italy produces olive oil, so there are many choices in the market. The quality is generally very high, so it's hard to go wrong when buying Italian olive oils. The best way to learn which you like is to taste as many of the available options as possible. If you're a first-time purchaser of a special extra-virgin olive oil, seek out a store that allows you to taste its oils before buying.

For the recipes in this book, use your favorite extra-virgin olive oil. You can use regular olive oil when high heat or a long cooking time would defeat the advantages of using expensive extra-virgin oil. When storing extra-virgin olive oil, keep the bottle in a cool, dark place.

pancetta and guanciale *Pancetta,* the belly meat of the pig, is rubbed with spices and rolled into a tight cylinder for curing, giving it a distinctive spiral of white fat when sliced. It is sometimes referred to as Italian bacon, although it is not smoked. Pancetta is used to flavor pasta sauces, meat dishes, and soups and stews.

Guanciale is meat from the pig's jowl and cheek. It is salted and cured and can be used like pancetta.

polenta

Polenta comes in three major varieties: yellow cornmeal, white cornmeal, and buckwheat. Yellow is the most common and has the most corn flavor. Yellow corn polenta takes a little longer than white to cook to the desired consistency, without "graininess"; the texture should be smooth, without detection of the individual polenta grain.

Polenta taragna, or buckwheat polenta, is actually equal parts yellow cornmeal and buckwheat flour. This is a heartier-flavored polenta that complements robust meats and game. This polenta is most popular in the northern alpine regions of Italy, such as Trentino and Alto Adige. A bowl of *polenta taragna* mixed with one of the region's cheeses—bitto or casera, for example—and some local sausage restores many a mountain climber or skier after a day on the slopes.

For a different wintertime accompaniment, try half yellow corn polenta and half chestnut flour. Garnish with some chopped roasted chestnuts and serve with roast pork or veal.

Polenta bianca, or white polenta, also referred to as *polenta bergamasca*, is a Venetian specialty and the preferred choice at Spiaggia for its surpassing softness and creaminess (see page 42). Moretti, from Bergamo in northern Italy, is our favorite brand. Cooked, cooled polenta can also be sliced and fried or grilled.

porcini mushrooms, dried

Porcini mushrooms, one of the most readily available types of wild mushroom in the United States—though usually in dried form—have an earthy, woodsy aroma and essence. They are often referred to as "the king of mushrooms" because of their size and flavor. Occasionally you can find fresh porcini, which have large, broad caps and chunky stems. Due to their firm and meaty texture, fresh porcini are perfect for the grill. In Italy, the stems are peeled and then shaved for salads.

To reconstitute dried porcini mushrooms, soak them in very hot water for about 20 minutes. Drain, reserving the soaking water, and rinse the mushrooms under cool water to wash away any clinging sediment. Reserve the mushroom soaking water to flavor sauces.

rice Italy produces more rice than any other European country and the most rice per acre of any place in the world. The only rice we use at Spiaggia is the Acquerello brand organic Carnaroli. It is the best rice for risotto because it consistently cooks up exceptionally creamy. Good substitutes for Carnaroli are Arborio and Vialone Nano. All three varieties have large grains and a high starch content, and they soak up liquid evenly while remaining firm, making them ideal for risotto.

sea salt Throughout this book, we encourage you to season to taste: your taste. It is the only true way of knowing how much seasoning is needed for a dish that you are preparing for you or your guests.

At Spiaggia, we have made fine sea salt our salt of choice because of its slightly coarse and crunchy texture and its pure flavor. Sea salt has no additives; it's an unadulterated distillate of sea water. It's also especially attractive when sprinkled on the finished plate.

tomatoes Of course, juicy fresh tomatoes in season are the tastiest. We use both regular and heirloom varietals, from local farms whenever possible. We recommend peeling and seeding tomatoes before using.

When tomatoes are out of season, look for imported canned Italian plum tomatoes, such as those grown in the volcanic soil around Mount Vesuvius in the area known as San Marzano. If unavailable, substitute the most natural canned tomatoes you can find, avoiding products containing citric acid and salt.

truffles Truffles are among the most exotic gifts of nature. They grow wild in Piemonte and Umbria in Italy and have a unique aroma and taste. They have been described variously as earthy, pungent, sexy, and luxurious. Truffles grow underground in symbiotic relationships with oak trees, poplars, and hazel bushes. In the past, truffle hunters, or *trifulau*, found their prizes with the help of a species of pig with a keen sense of smell; today most use specially trained mixed-breed dogs that learn the job faster than pigs, and tend to be easier to convince to trade a truffle for a biscuit.

The white truffle, also known as the Alba truffle after its area of origin, is the most sought-after truffle in the world. Fresh white truffles are best when thinly shaved over risotto, pasta, eggs, and raw beef. They have a powerful and earthy aroma of ripe cheese and garlic, and are available only from late October through late December. Black truffles come from Umbria, in the area around the town of Norcia. They have a bumpy exterior and when sliced reveal a marbled gray interior. Their aroma and flavor are subtle when compared to white truffles. At Spiaggia, we cook primarily with Norcia black truffles, mainly in sauces and pasta fillings.

For the recipes in this book, we recommend using truffle paste and truffle oil in dressings and sauces when fresh truffles are unavailable.

Italian Wine and Spiaggia

Drinking wine with meals is a ritual that Italians have practiced for centuries, so we knew our attention to wine at Spiaggia needed to be thorough and thoughtful. Spiaggia's wine program began quite modestly. In 1984, our guests made their wine selections from a four-page, sixty-item, all-Italian wine list. At that time it was unthinkable that a new downtown restaurant with four-star aspirations would not carry Chateau Latour and BV Georges de Latour. Nonetheless, we steadfastly chose to promote the finest flavors from "the Boot" at a time when Italian wine was a cipher for much of the wine-drinking public.

Looking at that original list today, it holds its own reasonably well. It featured, as always, the smaller, artisanal growers, with many significant players in attendance: Ferrari, Jermann, Anselmi, Gaja, and Maculan. The prices ranged from ten dollars for the 1982 Vernaccia di San Gimignano from Falchini, to a whopping sixty-five dollars for the 1968 Taurasi from Mastroberardino.

Our goal was to show guests that Italian wine was more than Pinot Grigio and Chianti, for everyday wines as well as those for special events. The latter category was trickier; in the 1980s, many upscale Italian restaurant wine lists still relied on French wines for special-occasion offerings. We created a separate *Riserva Speciale* card after we accumulated enough selections of unique and older vintages of red wines through auctions and from cellars in Italy.

This card was eventually incorporated into the list with the addition of what would be considered nontraditional descriptions by Spiaggia's sommelier, Henry Bishop III.

Henry was described in the Italian magazine *Civita del Bere* as "*il sommelier più pazzo nel mondo*," or "the craziest sommelier in the world." In addition to his colorful writings on wine, Henry displayed his "craziness" by following the growing interest in the cultivation of Italian varieties in California. He then expanded Spiaggia's wine list to include a category for these so-called Cal-Itals. The initial selection included a dry Malvasia Bianca from Randall Grahm's Ca' del Solo line, a Rosato di Aleatico from Benziger's Imagery Series, and a Nebbiolo from Jim Clendenen's Il Podere dell'Olivos brand.

Our guests had so much fun with the Cal-Ital program that we next pursued a sort of reverse manifest destiny by setting out north and east to acquire any quality American recapitulations of Italian varieties. It was especially gratifying to discover examples from the Midwest and to travel to the source and meet the winemakers. The program currently includes an Ohio Pinot Grigio from grapes grown on an island in the middle of Lake Erie and made by Claudio Saladore at Firelands in Sandusky; a Michigan Dolcetto grown and produced by Madonna's father, Tony Ciccone, at Suttons Bay; and a Virginian *vin santo* crafted by Lorenzo Zonin at Barboursville Vineyards, near Charlottesville. Feeling giddy from conquest, like Roman legionnaires, we then crossed international borders to acquire a Canadian Pinot Grigio from Mission Hill in the Okanagan Valley of British Columbia and a Mexican Nebbiolo from L. A. Cetto in the Valle de Guadalupe.

Meanwhile, annual shopping trips to Italy scheduled around the Vinitaly wine fair in Verona every April continue to introduce new regions, new producers, and new varieties to the list, as well as helping to keep a stock of antique vintages that presently contains bottles dating back to the classic 1931 harvest.

After visiting the Italian-speaking Ticino region of southern Switzerland, we felt compelled to add a section for these wines to our "Italian" list. Many Italian wine guides include a chapter about Ticino, albeit usually at the back of the book. Closer scrutiny reminded us that all of Italy's northern borders share a similarly symbiotic relationship with the other side, so more recently, we expanded the category to welcome Wines from the Neighborhood. This category now includes French wines from the island of Corsica, Bellet in eastern Provence, and alpine Bugey and Savoie. Other Swiss wines from the Valais and Vaud are also happily included. Austria's recent viticultural advances are welcome, as are the elusive flavors former Yugoslavia provides in Slovenian and Croatian inflections.

And so, over the past two decades, our fledgling *piccolo carta dei vini* has grown into an oversized leather-bound volume of forty pages with an average of six hundred selections representing Italy, its impact on its neighbors, and its influence on North American viticulture.

Our growth reflects a marketplace where the options for quality Italian wine have also grown for the average consumer. Italy produces more wine than any other nation on the "Third Vineyard from the Sun." Ampelographers (botanists who study grape varieties) recognize at least three thousand native Italian grape types. A recent government census reveals that there are 21,246 commercial wineries in the country. Vines grow everywhere from the Dolomitic northern borders to the warmer Mediterranean coasts. There is more wine to taste than ever before.

Italian wines are named in one of three different ways: for their grape type, for the place where the grapes are grown, or with an idiosyncratic Italian name given it by the winemaker. This can make buying Italian wine confusing. Sometimes the exact wine you are looking for falls into one of these categories.

When buying Italian wine, you should seek out a store that offers good, current selections, has a knowledgeable staff to assist you, and allows you to taste and/or offers wine tastings. Have fun; reputable wine shops love to help customers who ask questions. Good salespeople will tell you what's new and help you find a wine you will enjoy.

That's exactly what we do for our guests when they come to Spiaggia, and Henry does it with a special flair. For example, if a guest contemplating the white truffle menu isn't sure of which wine to choose, Henry might say, "If you have never experienced a venerable Barolo with white truffles, God will give you an 'Incomplete' when you reach the other side."

Basic Recipes

These recipes are elemental to several of the wonderful dishes served at Spiaggia. Most can be kept on hand (see recipe Notes) and used for more than one recipe, and the yields have been calculated with this in mind.

brodo di pollo

CHICKEN STOCK

This is our recipe for what we call "liquid gold." Use chicken backs and necks whenever possible; some butchers keep them on hand, while others will save them for you if you call ahead. Chicken wings and drumsticks also make good stock. oo **makes about 2 quarts**

4 pounds chicken parts	3 large stalks celery, cut into chunks
1 small yellow onion, coarsely chopped	2 bay leaves
3 small carrots, cut into chunks	1 teaspoon peppercorns, lightly crushed

Place the chicken in a large stockpot and add cold water to cover by 3 inches. Bring to a simmer over medium-high heat, skimming the stock of any fat or foam that rises to the surface. Add the onion, carrots, celery, bay leaves, and peppercorns.

Reduce heat to low and simmer, uncovered, for 2 to 3 hours. Strain through a fine-mesh sieve and let cool. Refrigerate overnight. With a large spoon, lift off and discard any solidified fat.

note oo The stock can be frozen for up to 1 month. Freezing it in ice-cube trays makes it easy to use for small-portion recipes.

brodo di vitello

VEAL STOCK

When making this stock, use veal neck bones if possible. If they are not readily available,
call your butcher in advance and request them, or use a combination of veal and beef bones.
o o makes about 2 quarts

4 tablespoons olive oil	3 large stalks celery, cut into chunks
4 pounds veal bones	1 tablespoon tomato paste
2 cups water	2 bay leaves
1 yellow onion, cut into chunks	1 teaspoon peppercorns, lightly crushed
3 carrots, cut into chunks	

Preheat the oven to 425 degrees F.

In a large roasting pan, combine 2 tablespoons of the olive oil and the veal bones.
Roast, turning every 15 minutes, until well browned, 45 to 60 minutes. When the bones
are nicely browned, transfer to a large stockpot. Set the roasting pan aside to cool. Add
cold water to the stockpot to cover the veal bones by 3 inches and bring to a simmer
over medium-high heat, skimming the stock of any fat or foam that rises to the surface.

Meanwhile, pour off any excess fat from the roasting pan, and place on the stovetop
over medium-high heat. When the pan is hot, add the 2 cups water and scrape the browned
bits off the bottom of the pan. Add the liquid to the stockpot with the veal bones.

Return the roasting pan to medium-high heat and add the remaining 2 tablespoons olive
oil. Add the onion, carrots, and celery and sauté until lightly browned, about 10 minutes.
Add the tomato paste, bay leaves, and peppercorns and cook until the vegetables are
softened and the flavors have blended, about 15 minutes. Add to the stockpot. Return
the stock to the stove, reduce the heat to low, and simmer, uncovered, for about 3
hours. Strain the stock through a fine-mesh sieve and let cool. Refrigerate overnight.
With a large spoon, lift off and discard any solidified fat. The stock is ready to use, or
bring it to a boil and reduce it further for a more concentrated stock.

notes o o Look for imported Italian tomato paste that comes in a tube, like toothpaste.
o o The stock can be frozen for up to 1 month.

salsa di spiaggia

SPIAGGIA DRESSING

The combination of brown butter and truffle oil is the secret behind our signature vinaigrette. It shines on warm shellfish and seafood dishes, too. ○○ **makes 1 cup**

2 tablespoons unsalted butter	Sea salt
2 tablespoons sherry vinegar	2 tablespoons truffle oil
2 tablespoons balsamic vinegar	½ cup extra-virgin olive oil

In a small saucepan over medium heat, melt the butter. Cook to a nutty brown color, until the foam subsides, 4 to 6 minutes. Remove from the heat and let cool to room temperature, about 20 minutes.

Meanwhile, in a bowl, combine the vinegars and salt to taste. Drizzle in the cooled brown butter and then the oils, whisking until the dressing is well blended. Season to taste.

note ○○ The dressing can be refrigerated for up to 1 week. Return to room temperature before using.

salsa di sherry

SHERRY VINAIGRETTE

This versatile dressing is a nice change on salad and shellfish. ○○ **makes 1⅓ cups**

1 small shallot, minced	⅛ teaspoon sea salt
½ teaspoon sugar	⅛ teaspoon freshly ground white pepper
⅓ cup sherry vinegar	1 cup extra-virgin olive oil

In a bowl, combine the shallot, sugar, vinegar, salt, and white pepper and stir until the sugar is dissolved. In a slow stream, drizzle in the olive oil, whisking constantly until the vinaigrette is well blended. Taste and adjust the seasoning.

note ○○ The dressing will keep at room temperature, away from light and heat, for up to 1 week.

salsa di balsamico

BALSAMIC VINAIGRETTE

This vinaigrette suits all types of salad greens, but for use with a mixture of sweet and bitter lettuces, there is none better. o o makes 1⅓ cups

¼ teaspoon sugar

⅓ cup balsamic vinegar

¼ teaspoon dry mustard

⅛ teaspoon sea salt

⅛ teaspoon freshly ground white pepper

1 cup extra-virgin olive oil

In a bowl, combine the sugar and vinegar and stir until the sugar is dissolved. Add the mustard, salt, and white pepper and mix well to combine. In a slow stream, drizzle in the olive oil, whisking constantly until the vinaigrette is well blended. Taste and adjust the seasoning.

note o o The vinaigrette will keep at room temperature, away from light and heat, for up to 1 week.

salsa di limone

LEMON VINAIGRETTE

We love this vinaigrette with raw fish because it is simple and refreshing. It is also a great dressing for grilled fish and seafood salads. o o makes ¾ cup

3 tablespoons fresh lemon juice

Pinch of sea salt

Pinch of freshly ground white pepper

½ cup plus 1 tablespoon extra-virgin olive oil

In a bowl, combine the lemon juice with the salt and white pepper. In a slow stream, drizzle in the olive oil, whisking constantly until the vinaigrette is well blended. Taste and adjust the seasoning.

note o o The vinaigrette can be refrigerated for up to 1 week. Return to room temperature before using.

liquido di cottura frutti di mare

SEAFOOD POACHING LIQUID

We like to poach seafood because it highlights natural flavors while keeping the texture firm. ○○ makes 2½ cups

2 cups water

¼ cup extra-virgin olive oil

¼ cup unsalted butter

1 cup loosely packed fresh basil leaves

5 sprigs fresh rosemary, each about 4 inches long

Sea salt and freshly ground white pepper

In a large saucepan over medium heat, combine the water, olive oil, butter, basil, rosemary, and salt and white pepper to taste. Heat, stirring occasionally, until the butter is melted and the poaching liquid is hot but not boiling. Use immediately.

sciroppo di balsamico

BALSAMIC REDUCTION

Reducing balsamic vinegar intensifies its flavor and sweetness, and the thickness of the reduced vinegar adds to its appeal as a garnish. ○○ makes ¾ cup

1½ cups balsamic vinegar

In a small saucepan over medium heat, bring the vinegar to a boil. Reduce the heat to medium-low and simmer until reduced by half, about 45 minutes. Let cool.

note ○○ Store in a small plastic squeeze bottle with a sealable top. The reduction will keep at room temperature, away from light and heat, for up to 6 months.

olio di basilico

BASIL OIL

You must blanch the basil first in order to retain its vibrant color in this versatile, fresh-flavored oil. ○○ makes 1 cup

| 4 cups loosely packed fresh basil leaves | 1 cup extra-virgin olive oil, slightly chilled |

Have ready a bowl of ice water. Bring a saucepan of water to a boil over high heat. Add the basil and blanch quickly, just a few seconds. Drain and plunge the wilted basil immediately into the ice water to stop the cooking. Drain and squeeze out additional moisture; the basil should be as dry as possible.

Transfer the basil to a food processor and process to a smooth paste, about 2 minutes, stopping to scrape down the sides of the jar or bowl as needed. With the motor running, slowly add the olive oil in a fine stream and process until emulsified, 2 to 3 minutes longer.

Strain the oil through a double thickness of cheesecloth into an airtight container and refrigerate until ready to use or for up to 2 weeks. Return to room temperature before using.

note ○○ The basil oil can be frozen for up to 1 month.

olio di dragoncello

TARRAGON OIL

Tarragon is an herb not normally associated with Italian cooking. At Spiaggia we use it sparingly, reserving it for certain dishes; we think its bright licorice flavor complements lobster more than any other herb. ○○ makes ¼ cup

Follow the method for Basil Oil (above), using 1 cup tarragon leaves and ¼ cup extra-virgin olive oil.

notes ○○ This oil can be made in a mini processor. ○○ Tarragon oil can be refrigerated for up to 2 weeks. Return to room temperature before using.

pesto alla genovese

LIGURIAN PESTO

In August, when fresh basil is abundant, make an extra batch of this pesto without the cheese and freeze it for a taste of summer on a cold winter's day. Add the cheese to the sauce when ready to use. ○○ makes 1 cup

2 cups loosely packed fresh basil leaves

1 clove garlic, chopped

3 tablespoons pine nuts

½ teaspoon sea salt

⅓ cup grated Romano cheese

⅓ cup grated Parmigiano-Reggiano or Parmesan cheese

3 to 4 tablespoons extra-virgin olive oil

In a blender or food processor, combine the basil, garlic, pine nuts, and salt. Process, stopping to scrape down the sides of the jar or bowl as needed, until the basil is finely chopped. Add the cheeses gradually, processing to a coarse paste.

With the motor running, slowly add the olive oil in a fine stream and process until the pesto is smooth and creamy.

note ○○ The pesto can be frozen for up to 1 month.

salsa di vitello

VEAL SAUCE

This sauce is rich and satisfying on its own, and can also be used as a base sauce for many dishes. By adding a different blend of herbs or substituting port or Madeira for the white wine, you can create a completely different sauce. After customizing the seasonings, consider finishing with an ingredient that also pairs well with what you're cooking. Everyone will want to know your secret to creating such delicious sauces. Because this sauce is so versatile, we recommend that you make plenty and freeze it in small containers for up to 1 month. ○○ **makes 3 to 4 cups**

½ cup extra-virgin olive oil

1 pound veal trimmings or veal stew meat, cut into 1-inch cubes

1 yellow onion, coarsely chopped

½ cup coarsely chopped celery

½ cup peeled and coarsely chopped carrot

1 whole head of garlic, cut in half

2 tablespoons tomato paste

2 cups dry white wine

1 bay leaf

2 quarts Veal Stock (page 33)

4 sprigs fresh thyme

2 sprigs fresh rosemary

8 peppercorns

In a large, heavy saucepan over medium-high heat, heat the olive oil until hot but not smoking. Add the veal and brown well on all sides, about 20 minutes. Reduce the heat to medium. Add the onion, celery, carrot, and garlic and cook until the onion is softened and caramelized, about 10 minutes.

Add the tomato paste and cook until it begins to caramelize, about 3 minutes. Add the wine and bay leaf, bring to a simmer, and cook until the liquid is reduced to about ¼ cup, 8 to 10 minutes. Add the stock, thyme, rosemary, and peppercorns and return to a simmer. Cook until the liquid is reduced by half or until it coats the back of a spoon, about 20 minutes.

Strain the sauce through a fine-mesh sieve, pressing on the solids with the back of a spoon.

Keep warm, covered, until ready to use, or let cool and refrigerate for up to 5 days.

salsa verde

SALSA VERDE

This Piemontese recipe incorporates hard-boiled egg, adding texture to a flavorful herb sauce traditionally served with fish and broiled meats. We like it with grilled chicken and vegetables, too. ○○ makes ⅔ cup

½ cup minced fresh tarragon

½ cup minced fresh chives

⅓ cup minced fresh flat-leaf (Italian) parsley

1 hard-boiled egg, peeled and chopped

½ teaspoon Dijon mustard

⅓ cup extra-virgin olive oil

1½ tablespoons capers, rinsed, drained, and chopped

In a bowl, combine the tarragon, chives, parsley, egg, mustard, olive oil, and capers. Stir to mix thoroughly and let stand for at least 1 hour to allow the flavors to blend.

note ○○ The sauce can be refrigerated for up to 1 week.

salsa al marzemino

MARZEMINO WINE SAUCE

Marzemino grapes yield a fruity and robust wine that we use to add a dimension of flavor to this sauce. If you can't find Marzemino, substitute another fruity red wine such as Chianti, Pinot Noir, or Merlot; be sure to choose one that you like to drink. ○○ makes about 2 cups

1 tablespoon butter, plus 1 cup unsalted butter, cut into small pieces

¼ cup minced shallots

5 sprigs fresh thyme

8 peppercorns

1½ cups Marzemino wine

1½ tablespoons heavy cream

Sea salt

In a saucepan over medium heat, melt the 1 tablespoon butter. Add the shallots, thyme, and peppercorns and cook until the shallots are translucent, 4 to 5 minutes.

Add the wine, bring to a simmer, and cook until reduced by half, 10 to 15 minutes.

Strain through a fine-mesh sieve, return to the pan, and place over very low heat. Whisk in the cream. Remove from the stove and whisk in the 1 cup butter, a few pieces at a time. Season to taste with salt. Serve immediately.

polenta bianca

WHITE CORN POLENTA

The following polenta recipes are included as a starch on our main plates. At Spiaggia, we serve polenta that has a creamy consistency, usually white corn polenta because it is the lightest and most elegant variety.

When you make white corn polenta, the finished texture should be that of runny mashed potatoes or very creamy risotto. You should be able to pour the polenta; it should actually relax onto the plate and then spread out slightly, but not too far. If the polenta stands up like whipped cream, you need to add more water or stock to achieve the desired consistency. Always taste and adjust the seasoning after adding more liquid. ○○ makes 2 cups

2 cups water

Sea salt

½ cup white polenta

1 tablespoon unsalted butter

6 tablespoons heavy cream

3 tablespoons grated Parmigiano-Reggiano or Parmesan cheese

Freshly ground white pepper

In a large saucepan over medium heat, bring the water to a boil. Add a pinch of salt and slowly pour in the polenta, stirring constantly to avoid any lumps. (Crush any lumps that form by pressing them against the side of the pot with a spoon.) Stir vigorously as the polenta thickens. Continue to cook the polenta, stirring often, until it loses its grainy texture and becomes smooth, about 30 minutes. Add the butter, cream, and Parmesan and stir until well incorporated. Season to taste with salt and white pepper. Serve immediately.

variation / **Buckwheat Polenta** / Follow the White Corn Polenta recipe (above), using ¼ cup white polenta and ¼ cup buckwheat polenta.

purea di patate

BASIC POTATO PURÉE

We prefer the creamy texture and taste of Yukon Gold potatoes for our purées.
○○ makes about 4 cups

1½ pounds Yukon Gold potatoes, peeled and quartered

¼ cup unsalted butter, at room temperature

½ cup heavy cream, warmed

Sea salt and freshly ground white pepper

Bring a large saucepan of lightly salted water to a boil. Add the potatoes, reduce the heat to a simmer, and cook until tender, 15 to 20 minutes. Drain the potatoes and return to the pan. Place over low heat until all excess water is gone, 2 to 3 minutes. Pass the potatoes through a ricer into a warmed bowl or transfer to the bowl and mash by hand with a potato masher. Fold in the butter and cream. Season to taste with salt and pepper. Serve immediately.

variations / **Black Truffle Potato Purée** / Prepare the Basic Potato Purée (above), then fold in 3 tablespoons black truffle paste and 1½ teaspoons white truffle oil. **Purple Potato Purée** / Prepare the Basic Potato Purée (above), using 1½ pounds purple potatoes in place of the Yukon Gold potatoes.

la pasta

BASIC PASTA DOUGH

We have tried many pasta dough recipes and have found this to be the best, yielding a firm dough with a texture that's easy to handle. Use this dough for all shapes and sizes of pasta. ○○ makes about 1 pound pasta dough, or twelve 6-by-12-inch sheets

2 cups type 00 semolina flour (see page 22)　　8 egg yolks, lightly beaten

1 teaspoon salt　　⅓ cup water

Mound the flour on a pastry board or other wood or plastic work surface. Make a well in the center and add the salt and egg yolks. Using a fork, gradually fold the flour into the eggs, adding the water little by little until you have a soft dough. Knead a few times until smooth, then form the dough into a ball, wrap in plastic, and refrigerate for 1 hour.

To roll and cut pasta, cut the dough into 6 pieces. Working with one piece at a time (cover the remaining dough with a moist cloth until ready to use), dust the dough with flour and place between the rollers of a manual or motorized pasta machine at the widest setting. Pass the dough through. Fold the dough in half, sprinkle with flour, and roll again. Dust again with flour if the dough becomes sticky. Continue this process, reducing the space between the rollers one setting at a time, until the dough is a thin, smooth sheet. Generally, you can roll the dough 6 times on the first setting before tightening the rollers; then reduce the times you roll by one with each new setting until you reach the last setting (No. 6), when rolling once will be enough.

The finished pasta sheets should be about 6 inches wide and 12 inches long. Let the pasta sheets dry on a lightly floured board or parchment paper for 5 minutes before cutting.

notes ○○ The basic pasta dough can be refrigerated, wrapped in plastic, for up to 2 days. ○○ When rolling dough for *corzetti* (page 85), roll the dough only to the No. 5 setting on the pasta machine; *corzetti* should be slightly thicker than other pasta. ○○ This recipe works well when cut in half, if you need less pasta. ○○ Most of Spiaggia's pasta recipes call for fresh pasta. Nowadays, fairly inexpensive manual and electric pasta machines and electric roller and cutter attachments for stand mixers make preparing fresh pasta easy for the home cook.

salsa di lamponi

RASPBERRY SAUCE

Make this sauce in the spring when raspberries are at their sweet, juicy best.
○○ makes about 4 cups

3 pints fresh or frozen raspberries

2 cups sugar

½ cup dry white wine

¼ cup water

In a heavy-bottomed saucepan over medium-high heat, combine the raspberries, sugar, wine, and water. Bring the mixture to a boil, about 5 minutes. Let cool slightly, then transfer to a blender and process to a purée. Strain the purée through a fine-mesh sieve. Chill overnight.

note ○○ The sauce can be frozen for up to 1 month.

panna montata

WHIPPED CREAM

We generally use whipped cream without added sugar in our desserts; however, here's an all-purpose slightly sweetened recipe. Use less sugar, if you like, or leave out the sugar altogether.
○○ makes 4 cups

2 cups heavy cream, chilled

2 tablespoons sugar

Using an electric mixer on medium speed, beat the cream in a chilled bowl until it begins to thicken. Add the sugar in a steady stream and continue to beat until the cream forms medium to stiff peaks.

note ○○ The whipped cream can be refrigerated for up to 2 hours.

GLI ANTIPASTI appetizers and salads

○ ○ ○ *ANTIPASTO* IS A WORD MOST AMERICANS RECOGNIZE AS THE PLATTERS OF CHEESES, CURED MEATS, AND VEGETABLES THAT APPEAR ON SEVERAL ITALIAN RESTAURANT MENUS IN THE STATES. IN FACT, THROUGHOUT ITALY *ANTIPASTI* INCLUDE ALL KINDS OF STARTER DISHES TO STIMULATE THE TASTE BUDS IN PREPARATION FOR THE COURSES TO FOLLOW.

AFTER MANY YEARS OF DEVELOPING CREATIVE *ANTIPASTI*, SPIAGGIA'S SEAFOOD AND SHELLFISH APPETIZERS ARE STILL OUR MOST POPULAR. WITH THE PHENOMENON OF OVERNIGHT SHIPPING, ALL KINDS OF SEAFOOD THAT WERE SWIMMING IN THE MEDITERRANEAN SEA ONE MORNING CAN BE DELIVERED TO THE RESTAURANT AND SERVED THE NEXT DAY. NOW WE HAVE ACCESS TO PRODUCTS THAT AT ONE TIME WERE IMPOSSIBLE TO GET FRESH OR TO GET AT ALL.

MAKING *ANTIPASTI* BRINGS OUT THE PLAYFUL NATURE OF THE SPIAGGIA KITCHEN TEAM. WE LIKE TO COMBINE CONTRASTING TASTES AND TEXTURES FOR AN ELEMENT OF SURPRISE. ELEGANCE ISN'T STUFFY AT SPIAGGIA.

insalatina di cappesante dorate

GOLDEN SCALLOPS SALAD

The fresh flavor of the ingredients makes this easy-to-prepare dish one of Spiaggia's winning first courses. Purchase sea scallops out of the shell labeled "diver caught" or "dry pack"; this refers to scallops that are caught by hand and not packed in water. If your fishmonger sells only scallops in water, drain the scallops and pat dry with paper towels to remove the excess moisture prior to cooking, ensuring a firmer scallop and better browning. ○ o serves 4

2 ounces dried (or 4 ounces fresh) sliced porcini mushrooms (see Notes)

4 ounces fresh mushrooms, such as shiitakes, chanterelles, or portobellos, brushed clean

5 tablespoons extra-virgin olive oil

12 medium diver-caught sea scallops (see recipe introduction)

4 cups mâche lettuce, cleaned and dried, plus extra leaves for garnish (see Notes)

Sea salt and freshly ground pepper

¾ cup Spiaggia Dressing (page 34)

12 pieces shaved Parmigiano-Reggiano or Parmesan cheese

Place the dried porcini in a bowl with very hot water to cover. Soak for about 20 minutes, then drain and rinse. Thinly slice the fresh mushrooms.

In a skillet over medium heat, heat 2 tablespoons of the olive oil. Add all the mushrooms and sauté until lightly browned and tender, 5 to 7 minutes. Transfer to a small bowl and cover to keep warm.

In the same skillet over medium-high heat, heat the remaining 3 tablespoons olive oil. Add the scallops and cook, turning once, until golden brown on the outside and opaque throughout, 2 to 3 minutes per side. Transfer to a plate.

In a bowl, toss the mâche with salt and pepper to taste. Divide the warm mushrooms evenly among 4 plates and place 3 scallops on top of the mushrooms. Arrange the mâche around the scallops. Drizzle each serving with the dressing and garnish with 3 cheese shavings. Top each with extra mâche leaves and serve immediately.

notes ○ o Porcini mushrooms, also known as *cèpes,* have a meaty texture and wonderful, earthy flavor. At Spiaggia, we use imported fresh porcini mushrooms for this dish. Fresh porcini are often very difficult to find in American markets, however, so we call for dried here, as they are readily available and also have excellent flavor. If you do find fresh porcini, by all means use them instead. ○○ Mâche, also know as lambs lettuce, is characterized by its bright green rounded leaves. It has a delicate, nutty flavor. If your market does not offer mâche, you can substitute watercress or mixed baby salad greens.

insalatina di astice alla catalana

LOBSTER SALAD WITH ARUGULA, TOMATO, AND SWEET ONION

The west coast of the island of Sardinia faces Catalonia, and throughout the island you sense the influence of Spain in much of the cooking. This very popular dish illustrates how the cooking there differs from the rest of the Italian peninsula.

In Sardinia, *carta da musica,* a thin, crispy flat bread, is typically used in this dish. Flat breads and thin cracker breads are now available in most supermarkets and make a fine substitute for the Italians' "music paper." Just make sure that the bread or cracker you choose is thin and crispy.

○ ○ serves 4

2 live Maine lobsters, about 1½ pounds each

4 ounces fresh arugula leaves

¼ cup thinly sliced Vidalia or other sweet onion

½ cup Sherry Vinaigrette (page 34)

Purchased crispy flat bread or cracker bread for serving (see recipe introduction)

½ cup quartered cherry tomatoes

Sea salt

½ ounce lobster caviar (optional; see Notes)

Freshly ground pepper

Have ready a large bowl of ice water. Bring a large pot of salted water to a boil. Add the lobsters, head first, and cook, covered, for 10 to 12 minutes, counting the cooking time from the moment you add them to the pot. Transfer to the ice bath and let cool. When cool enough to handle, remove the claws by twisting and pulling. Carefully crack the claws open and remove the claw meat intact. Set the whole claw meats aside. Split the lobster lengthwise and pull the tail meat out of the shell. Remove and discard the dark intestine that runs the length of the tail. Cut the tail meat into bite-sized pieces. (If you prefer not to cook the lobster yourself, any seafood store that sells live lobsters will steam them for you. Ask them to remove the shells, leaving the meat as intact as possible, especially the claw meat.)

In a large bowl, combine the lobster tail meat, arugula, onion, and ¼ cup of the vinaigrette and toss gently. Divide half of the lobster salad among 4 chilled plates.

Break the flat bread into 8 shards, each about 2 inches wide and 4 inches long. Layer 2 shards on each salad to create more height. Divide the remaining salad atop the flat bread.

Place a few tomato pieces and 1 claw meat section on top of each salad. Sprinkle 1 tablespoon of the remaining ¼ cup vinaigrette and a pinch of sea salt over each serving of tomatoes and claw. Spoon a generous teaspoon of lobster caviar on top, if using. Serve immediately. Pass freshly ground pepper at the table.

notes ○○ This salad tastes best when the sweetness of the lobster, onion, and tomatoes plays off the peppery, slightly bitter arugula. If you prefer a milder salad, however, you can substitute mixed salad greens. ○○ At Spiaggia we like to use lobster caviar for this dish, not only for the flavor, but also for its attractive color and size. It can be purchased through your fishmonger. You can substitute salmon caviar.

fegato di anitra con polenta bianca e mele cotogne con moscato

SEARED FOIE GRAS WITH WHITE CORN POLENTA AND QUINCE WITH PASSITO DI MOSCATO SYRUP

This is a very Italian preparation for duck or goose liver. Passito di Moscato is a dessert wine with an intense concentration of fruity *Moscato,* or muscat, wine flavor. Quince, a delicious fruit in the apple family, is only eaten cooked, not raw. ○o serves 4

2 cups Passito di Moscato wine
(see recipe introduction)

1 cup White Corn Polenta (page 42)

2 medium quinces, peeled and cut into ¼-inch dice

1 tablespoon unsalted butter

Sea salt and freshly ground pepper

8 ounces foie gras, cleaned and soaked (see page 22), then cut into quarters

2 teaspoons Aceto Balsamico Riserva (optional; see Notes)

In a small, heavy-bottomed saucepan, bring the wine to a boil over high heat. Reduce the heat to very low and cook until syrupy and reduced to about ¾ cup, about 1½ hours. Set aside and keep warm.

Make the polenta. Set aside and keep warm.

Put the quinces in a saucepan with water to cover and bring to a boil over medium-high heat. Cook until crisp-tender, 3 to 5 minutes. Drain and set aside. Melt the butter in the same pan over medium heat. Add the quinces and sauté until golden on all sides, 3 to 5 minutes. Season to taste with salt and pepper and set aside.

Season the foie gras with salt and pepper. In a sauté pan over high heat, sear the foie gras until golden on all sides and rare in the center, 1 to 2 minutes per side.

To serve, spoon an oval of polenta into the right-hand section of each of 4 plates. Divide the quince among the plates, arranging it next to the polenta. Put a piece of seared foie gras on top of the polenta and drizzle the *Moscato* syrup around each plate. Add a few drops of Aceto Balsamico Riserva, if using.

notes ○o If you cannot find Passito di Moscato, substitute any good sweet wine. The syrup can be made a day ahead and warmed before serving. ○o Aceto Balsamico Riserva is an intense, complex condiment and a perfect foil for the richness of foie gras.

It is somewhat expensive and hard to find, but the flavor is well worth the effort. Look for a bottle that has been aged at least 12 years. See Resources (page 186) for information on purchasing.

carne cruda all'albese

KOBE BEEF TARTAR WITH TRUFFLE, CELERY, AND PARMIGIANO-REGGIANO

Kobe beef, appreciated for its intense marbling, originated in the area of Kobe, Japan. The cattle breed used to produce Kobe beef is called Wagyu, and the animals are massaged with sake and fed large quantities of beer. The theory behind the massage is that a calm steer produces higher-quality beef, while the beer stimulates the appetite. Both these practices came about because of the limited space available in Japan for grazing. Wagyu cattle are now raised with similar practices in the United States. This beef, chopped and dressed with truffle paste, lemon, olive oil, and Parmigiano-Reggiano, is the kind of luxurious dish that our guests expect at Spiaggia.
○○ serves 4

6 ounces Kobe beef (see recipe introduction), very finely diced

1½ teaspoons white truffle oil

1 teaspoon white truffle paste

1 tablespoon freshly squeezed lemon juice

Sea salt and freshly ground white pepper

2 tablespoons finely diced celery

2 tablespoons extra-virgin olive oil

4 thin slices Parmigiano-Reggiano or Parmesan cheese

Julienned fresh celery leaves or microcelery (see Note) for garnish

In a bowl, combine the beef, truffle oil, truffle paste, lemon juice and salt and pepper to taste. Mix thoroughly.

In a separate bowl, dress the celery with 1 tablespoon of the olive oil and a pinch of salt and pepper.

Using a ring mold 1½ inches wide, cut a round out of each Parmigiano-Reggiano slice. Set aside.

Lightly oil the inside of a ring mold 2 inches tall and 1½ inches wide and place in the center of one of 4 plates. Fill the bottom with one-fourth of the dressed celery. Top with one-fourth of the beef mixture and press down gently to pack the layers. Carefully remove the ring mold, keeping the layers intact. Top the beef with a Parmigiano-Reggiano round. Repeat to make the remaining 3 servings. Garnish each serving with the celery leaves and drizzle the plates with the remaining 1 tablespoon olive oil.

note ○○ See Resources (page 186) for information on purchasing microcelery.

merluzzo ai due caviali

SPANISH MACKEREL WITH TWO CAVIARS

The mackerel served at sushi bars inspired this antipasto for Spiaggia. The apple balances the richness of mackerel nicely. You can replace pike and trout roes with a more traditional caviar such as sturgeon, or omit the roe altogether. (See photo page 58–right.) ○○ serves 4

4 ounces skinned mackerel fillets, finely diced

5 teaspoons Lemon Vinaigrette (page 35)

Sea salt and freshly ground pepper

2 tablespoons finely diced Granny Smith apple

½ ounce pike roe (optional)

½ ounce trout roe (optional)

In a bowl, combine the mackerel, 2 teaspoons of the vinaigrette, and salt and pepper to taste and toss to mix. In a small bowl, toss the apple with 1 teaspoon of the vinaigrette.

Lightly oil a ring mold 2 inches tall and 1½ inches wide, and place in the center of one of 4 plates. Spoon in one-fourth of the dressed apple. Top with one-fourth of the mackerel mixture and press down gently to pack the layers. Carefully remove the ring mold, keeping the layers intact. Place one-fourth of the pike roe on one-half of the top of the cylinder and one-fourth of the trout roe on the other, if using. Repeat to make the remaining 3 servings. Drizzle the remaining 2 teaspoons vinaigrette around the mackerel and serve.

pesce spada affumicato con avocado, caviale di osetra e gelatina di pomodoro fresco

SMOKED SWORDFISH WITH AVOCADO, OSETRA CAVIAR, AND FRESH TOMATO GELÉE

Smoked swordfish is a fairly common ingredient that deserves more attention. Cold smoked like salmon, it stays moist and tender. A drizzle of Sicilian olive oil, and the swordfish may think it's back home in the Strait of Messina. Avocado, though not a common Italian ingredient, complements both the swordfish and the caviar in this dish. Tomato gelée is a great way to capture the taste of fresh tomatoes. (See photo page 58–left.) ○○ serves 4

2 medium, ripe tomatoes

1 envelope unflavored gelatin (about 1½ teaspoons)

4 ounces smoked swordfish, finely diced

4 teaspoons extra-virgin olive oil

½ ripe avocado, pitted, peeled, and finely diced

1 tablespoon osetra caviar

Have ready a bowl of ice water. Bring a saucepan of water to a boil over medium-high heat. Core the top and cut an X into the bottom of each tomato. Add to the boiling water and blanch for 10 seconds. Drain and quickly plunge the tomatoes into the ice water. Let cool, then drain the tomatoes and peel off the skins. Transfer the peeled tomatoes to a food processor and process to a purée. Strain the purée through a fine-mesh sieve, pushing on the solids with the back of a spoon to extract as much juice as possible.

Lightly spray with canola oil a shallow heat-proof dish large enough so that the purée will spread into a thin layer. In a saucepan, bring the strained tomato purée to a simmer. Add the gelatin and stir to dissolve. Pour the warm gelatin mixture into the prepared dish. Top with plastic wrap and refrigerate until set, about 1 hour. Turn the set gelatin out onto a cutting board and use a 1½-inch ring mold to cut out 4 rounds.

To serve, dress the swordfish with the olive oil. Lightly oil a ring mold 2 inches tall and 1½ inches wide, and place in the center of one of 4 plates. Spoon in one-fourth of the avocado. Layer one-fourth of the swordfish over the avocado. Place a tomato gelatin round on top of the fish. Remove the ring mold carefully. Repeat to make the remaining 3 servings. Garnish each serving with the caviar and serve.

tartar di baccalà con peperoni arrostiti

SALT COD TARTAR WITH ROASTED PEPPERS

Baccalà, or salt cod, is found in kitchens all over the Mediterranean—in Italy, Spain, Greece, France, and Portugal. Cod is found in the Atlantic, not the Mediterranean, and in the past, northern Europeans traded the dried, salted fish with Mediterranean travelers in exchange for terra-cotta and other products of their region. The roaming southerners highly valued *baccalà.* (See photo page 59–right.) ○○ serves 4

2 ounces salt cod

½ red bell pepper, roasted (see page 75) and cut into thin strips

1 teaspoon minced shallot

4 teaspoons extra-virgin olive oil, plus extra for drizzling

Sea salt and freshly ground pepper

¼ cup mixed microgreens for garnish (see Note)

Soak the cod in cold water in the refrigerator for 2 days, changing the water every 4 to 8 hours. Drain. Cut into 4 equal slices.

In a bowl, toss together the roasted pepper, shallot, olive oil, and salt and pepper to taste.

To serve, lightly oil the inside of a ring mold 2 inches tall and 3 inches wide and place in the center of one of 4 plates. Spoon one-fourth of the pepper mixture into the mold and press gently to pack the layer. Top with a slice of the salt cod and press gently again. Carefully remove the ring mold, keeping the layers intact. Repeat to make the remaining 3 servings. Drizzle each serving with a tiny bit more olive oil. Garnish with the mixed microgreens and serve.

note ○○ See Resources (page 186) for information on purchasing microgreens.

filetto di hamachi crudo con olio di tartufo e caviale

SUSHI-GRADE YELLOWTAIL WITH TRUFFLE OIL AND CAVIAR

There is a surprising organic logic in pairing soy with truffle. High-quality sushi-grade yellowtail, or *hamachi,* is the perfect fish for these flavors. (See photo page 59–left.) ○○ **serves 4**

4 ounces sushi-grade yellowtail, finely diced

½ teaspoon white truffle paste

2 teaspoons white truffle oil

1 teaspoon Lemon Vinaigrette (page 35)

2 tablespoons diced celery

3 teaspoons extra-virgin olive oil

Sea salt and freshly ground pepper

2 teaspoons crème fraîche

1 ounce osetra caviar

1 teaspoon soy sauce

In a bowl, combine the yellowtail, truffle paste, 1 teaspoon of the truffle oil, and the vinaigrette. Toss gently to mix and set aside.

In another bowl, toss the celery with 2 teaspoons of the olive oil and salt and pepper to taste. Set aside.

To serve, place a lightly oiled ring mold 2 inches tall and 1½ inches wide in the center of one of 4 chilled plates. Spoon one-fourth of the dressed celery into the mold and press gently to pack the layer. Spoon in one-fourth of the yellowtail mixture and again press gently. Carefully remove the ring mold, keeping the layers intact. Repeat to make the remaining 3 servings. Garnish each serving with a dollop of crème fraîche and caviar.

Just before serving, in a small bowl, whisk together the soy sauce and the remaining 1 teaspoon truffle oil until emulsified. Pour a small amount of the soy-truffle dressing on one side of each plate. Drizzle the other side of each plate with the remaining 1 teaspoon olive oil.

polipo alla griglia con fagioli nani e capperi

GRILLED BABY OCTOPUS WITH RICE BEANS AND CAPERS

You can order whole baby octopus through most fishmongers. The best seafood suppliers will deliver the octopuses pretenderized with a special appliance; if yours are not, you may want to parboil them before grilling. Tiny rice beans, like lentils, do not require presoaking before cooking. They are available in well-stocked supermarkets and natural foods stores. ○○ serves 4

¼ cup rice beans, picked over and rinsed	¼ cup extra-virgin olive oil
¼ yellow onion	2 tablespoons capers, rinsed and drained
½ carrot, peeled	½ tablespoon chopped fresh chives
½ stalk celery	4 teaspoons diced red bell pepper
1 bay leaf	4 tablespoons Lemon Vinaigrette (page 35)
4 whole baby octopuses, 4 to 6 ounces each	Fresh arugula leaves for garnish

Place the beans in a saucepan with fresh water to cover by 3 inches. Add the onion, carrot, celery, and bay leaf and bring to a simmer over high heat. Reduce the heat to low and simmer until the beans are tender, 1 to 1½ hours. Drain and set aside. Discard the vegetables and the bay leaf.

Prepare a fire in a charcoal grill or preheat a gas grill to 400 degrees F.

In a bowl, coat the octopuses with the olive oil and let stand for 2 to 3 minutes. Drain and arrange on the grill. Cook, turning once or twice, until slightly charred on both sides and opaque throughout, 5 to 7 minutes. Slice each octopus into 8 tentacle pieces.

In a bowl, combine the capers, chives, red pepper, and rice beans and toss with 2 tablespoons of the vinaigrette.

To serve, divide the bean mixture into 8 equal portions. In the center of each of four 10-inch plates, place 3 octopus pieces in a circle. Spoon 1 portion of the bean mixture on top. Top with 3 more pieces and then another layer of beans. Repeat to make the remaining 3 servings.

Garnish each serving with 2 octopus pieces and drizzle the remaining vinaigrette around the octopus towers. Garnish each tower with arugula and serve.

scampi con fagiolini

LANGOUSTINOS WITH GREEN BEANS

In the summer of 1983, we had the incredible learning experience of working with Romano and Franca Franceschini and the impeccably fresh seafood at their restaurant, Da Romano, which inspired this dish. Traditionally, this salad is made with shrimp; we make it with langoustinos, Mediterranean crustaceans that look like small lobsters. ○ ○ serves 4

4 cups water

1 cup dry white wine

1 pound langoustino tails, shelled, or medium to large shrimp, shelled and deveined

8 ounces haricots verts or other young, tender green beans

¼ cup fresh cilantro leaves, plus extra for garnish

1 teaspoon coriander seeds, crushed, plus extra for garnish

¼ cup extra-virgin olive oil

Pinch of sea salt

In a heavy-bottomed saucepan, combine the water and wine and bring to a simmer over medium-high heat. Reduce the heat to medium, add the langoustino meat, and poach until opaque throughout, 2 to 3 minutes. Drain and set aside.

Have ready a bowl of ice water. Bring a saucepan of lightly salted water to a boil over medium-high heat. Add the beans and cook until crisp-tender but still vibrant green, 3 to 5 minutes. Drain and quickly plunge the beans into the ice water. Let cool completely, then drain again.

In a large bowl, toss together the beans, langoustino, the ¼ cup cilantro, the 1 teaspoon coriander, the olive oil, and salt. Divide the salad equally among 4 plates. Garnish with cilantro leaves and crushed coriander seeds and serve.

sarde marinate con patate e salsa verde

MARINATED SARDINES WITH ROASTED POTATOES AND SALSA VERDE

When it comes to sardines, generally people either like them or they don't, but when we serve this recipe to diners at Spiaggia who usually avoid sardines, they often say, "I love these!"
○○ serves 4

Sea salt

6 fresh sardines, filleted (see Note)

1 cup extra-virgin olive oil

1 cup fresh orange juice

½ cup white wine vinegar

2 cloves garlic, crushed

4 fingerling potatoes, unpeeled

4 tablespoons Salsa Verde (page 40)

4 caper berries for garnish

Salt the sardines and let stand for 10 minutes. In a bowl, whisk together ½ cup of the olive oil, the orange juice, and the vinegar. Put the sardines in a shallow dish and pour the marinade over. Marinate for 30 minutes, then remove the sardines from the marinade and lightly pat dry. Put the sardines in a clean shallow dish with the remaining ½ cup olive oil and scatter with the garlic cloves.

Place the potatoes in a saucepan with cold water to cover and a pinch of salt. Bring to a simmer and cook just until tender, about 10 minutes. Drain and let cool. When cool enough to handle, slice the potatoes into 24 disks and dress in a bowl with 2 table-spoons of the salsa verde.

To serve, arrange 6 potato disks on each of 4 plates. Remove 3 sardine fillets from the olive oil and shake off excess oil or any garlic. Lay the fillets on top of the potatoes. Repeat to make the remaining 3 servings. Garnish each serving with the caper berries and drizzle the remaining 2 tablespoons salsa verde around the plates.

note ○○ You can ask the fishmonger to fillet the sardines. Plan to use them within 24 hours of buying.

nocette di coniglio con carciofini

ROASTED RABBIT LOIN WITH BABY ARTICHOKES

This dish offers a delightful variety of tastes and textures: sweet, smoky, tart, juicy, crunchy, and tender. Rabbit loin is a white meat like chicken and has a mild taste. Wrapped with bacon, the meat bastes as it cooks. ○○ serves 4

2 lemons

12 baby artichokes

4 whole rabbit loins (see Notes)

2 teaspoons minced fresh rosemary

Sea salt and freshly ground pepper

4 thin slices bacon (see Notes)

1½ ounces caul fat (see page 21)

4 tablespoons extra-virgin olive oil

4 ounces fresh arugula, tough stems removed, with 8 leaves reserved for garnish

Balsamic Reduction (page 36) for serving

Preheat the oven to 450 degrees F. Bring a large saucepan three-fourths full of water to a boil.

Fill a large bowl with cold water. Cut one of the lemons in half and squeeze the juice into the bowl, then add the cut lemon halves. Cut off the stem and top one-fourth of one artichoke. Bend back and snap off the dark green outer leaves at the base until only the pale green and yellow leaves remain. Cut the artichoke in half lengthwise. Using the point of a knife, remove any purple-tipped leaves or fuzzy choke from the center, if necessary. Place the artichoke halves in the lemon water. Repeat with the remaining artichokes.

Squeeze the juice of the remaining lemon into the boiling water. Drain the artichokes, add to the boiling water, and blanch for 8 to 10 minutes. Drain and set aside.

Season the rabbit loins with the rosemary and salt and pepper to taste. Wrap a bacon piece around each loin. Cut the caul fat into 4 equal squares, then wrap each loin in a square of caul. Arrange the wrapped loins, seam side down, in a roasting pan and roast until just cooked through and browned on the edges, 10 to 12 minutes.

Meanwhile, cook the artichokes: In a sauté pan over high heat, heat 2 tablespoons of the olive oil. Add the artichokes and sauté until tender and the edges are browned and crispy, 2 to 3 minutes. Remove from the heat and drain off any excess oil.

continued ○○

Move the artichokes to the left side of the pan and add the arugula to the right. Using tongs, toss the arugula just until wilted.

Divide the arugula among the centers of 4 plates. Top each with 6 artichoke halves. Unwrap each rabbit loin and discard the caul. Cut each bacon-wrapped loin in half and then cut each half on the diagonal in half again (for a total of 4 pieces per loin). Place the rabbit on top of the artichokes and arugula. Drizzle with the remaining 2 tablespoons olive oil and dot each plate with drops of balsamic reduction. Garnish each with 2 arugula leaves. Serve immediately.

notes o o Quality rabbit is more readily available now than ever. If you cannot buy just the loin, ask the butcher to cut up a whole rabbit, keeping the loin and legs intact, and use the legs for another recipe (see our recipe for gnocchi with braised rabbit on page 93). o o When we use smoked pork products at Spiaggia, we prefer Nueske brand meats. Produced here in the Midwest, Nueske bacon is high quality, not overly fatty, and has a hearty apple-wood smoke flavor. See Resources (page 186) for information on purchasing Nueske bacon.

gamberoni rossi in salsa con purea di ceci

POACHED RED SHRIMP WITH SHRIMP SAUCE AND CHICKPEA PURÉE

This is a variation on a classic Italian flavor profile, shrimp and beans. The beans in this instance are chickpeas, also called *ceci* or garbanzo beans. They are puréed to create a light and creamy bean base.

The red shrimp in this dish are from the Mediterranean, and seeking them out is definitely worth the extra effort. Their flavor is very rich, more like lobster than shrimp. Often these shrimp are referred to as *carabinieri* shrimp, for their resemblance to the red plume on the dress hat of the Italian police, the *carabinieri*. The sauce is made from the shells of the shrimp, which you remove prior to cooking. Make it any time you are cooking with raw shrimp; there is so much flavor in these bits, it seems wrong to throw them away. ○○ serves 4

For the Chickpea Purée:

1 cup dried chickpeas, picked over, rinsed, and soaked in cold water to cover overnight

2 yellow onions, cut into quarters

3 carrots, peeled and cut into chunks

2 stalks celery, cut in half crosswise

1 head garlic, halved

2 or 3 sprigs fresh rosemary

For the Shrimp Sauce:

¼ cup olive oil

Shells from 8 large red shrimp (below)

½ cup peeled and diced carrot

½ cup diced celery

½ yellow onion, diced

3 tablespoons chopped garlic

½ cup brandy

1 cup dry white wine

2 tablespoons tomato paste

6 cups water

2 tablespoons unsalted butter

10 cups Seafood Poaching Liquid (page 36)

8 large red shrimp (see recipe introduction), heads on, shelled and deveined

Sea salt and freshly ground pepper

Extra-virgin olive oil for drizzling

continued ○○

To make the chickpea purée: Drain the beans. In a large stockpot, combine the drained beans, onions, carrots, celery, garlic, and rosemary. Add cold water to cover by 3 inches and bring to a boil over medium-high heat. Reduce the heat to medium-low and simmer, uncovered, stirring occasionally, until the beans are extremely soft, about 2 hours. Drain the beans and vegetables, reserving the liquid. Remove the large chunks of vegetables and the rosemary from the beans and discard. Transfer the beans to a food processor and purée, leaving the consistency on the thick side. If necessary, use some of the reserved cooking liquid to adjust to the desired consistency. Set aside.

While the beans are cooking, make the sauce: In a saucepan, heat the olive oil over medium-high heat. Add the shrimp shells and sauté until they turn deep red, about 10 minutes. Add the carrot, celery, onion, and garlic and cook until the onion is slightly caramelized, about 5 minutes longer. Add the brandy and white wine and scrape the browned bits off the bottom of the pan. Stir in the tomato paste and water, reduce the heat to low, and simmer until reduced by half, about 2 hours. Strain the sauce through a fine-mesh sieve, pressing on the solids with the back of a spoon. Return the sauce to the pan, bring just to a boil over medium-high heat, and cook to reduce by one-third. Remove from the heat and slowly whisk in the butter until emulsified into the sauce. Keep warm, covered, until ready to use.

Prepare the poaching liquid. Season the shrimp with salt and pepper. Add to the hot poaching liquid and poach gently until opaque throughout, about 2 minutes. Using a slotted spoon, transfer the shrimp to paper towels to drain.

To serve, divide the shrimp sauce among 4 individual plates. Spoon an oval of the chickpea purée on top of the sauce in the middle of each plate. With the heads up, arrange 2 shrimp leaning on the chickpea purée. Drizzle each serving with extra-virgin olive oil, sprinkle with sea salt, and serve.

mozzarella di bufala con peperoni arrostiti, carciofi, olive cerignola e pesto

FRESH MOZZARELLA CHEESE WITH ROASTED PEPPERS, ARTICHOKES, CERIGNOLA OLIVES, AND LIGURIAN PESTO

This recipe has become the seasonal alternative for Spiaggia's version of *insalata caprese,* a delightful summer salad of heirloom tomatoes, fresh basil, and fresh mozzarella. ○○ serves 4

4 small red or yellow bell peppers (see Notes)

¼ cup Ligurian Pesto (page 38)

4 ounces fresh mozzarella cheese, cut into 4 equal pieces

8 halves dry-packed sun-dried tomato, puréed with 2 tablespoons olive oil, or 4 tablespoons purchased sun-dried tomato purée

4 long-stemmed marinated Italian artichoke halves (see Notes), or one 5-ounce jar marinated artichokes, drained

12 brine-packed Cerignola olives, drained

2 tablespoons extra-virgin olive oil

2 tablespoons Basil Oil (page 37)

4 fresh basil leaves for garnish

To roast the peppers, using tongs or a long fork, hold a pepper directly in the flame of a gas burner, turning as needed to char the pepper evenly on all sides. (Alternatively, preheat the broiler and roast the pepper on the broiler pan.) When the skin is blackened and blistered all over, transfer the pepper to a paper bag or bowl. Repeat with the remaining peppers. Seal the bag or cover the bowl tightly with plastic wrap and let the peppers steam for about 10 minutes. When the peppers are cool enough to handle, peel off the charred skins.

Place a small pool of pesto in the center of each of 4 plates. Place the mozzarella pieces on top. Place a small oval of 1 tablespoon sun-dried tomato purée on top of the mozzarella. Arrange the marinated artichokes next to the mozzarella, along with the roasted peppers and the olives. Drop alternate sprinkles of olive oil and basil oil around each plate. Garnish each serving with a basil leaf.

notes ○○ Look for small bell peppers called Tinkerbell peppers, about 2 inches wide and 2 inches high. If unavailable, use the smallest bell peppers you can find, or substitute 8 slices of purchased roasted peppers. ○○ Our favorite artichokes for this dish are imported by Sid Wainer & Son; see Resources (page 186) for more information.

cardi con fonduta

CARDOONS WITH FONTINA CHEESE SAUCE

Cardoons are typically a southern Italian vegetable, while *fonduta* is a northern Italian recipe. Here, south meets north, "poor" vegetable meets the "richness" of fontina.

Cardoons are sort of like prehistoric celery, but with the flavor of artichokes. You must carefully remove the tough fibrous strings that run down the outer edge of each stalk. As soon as the stalks are trimmed, put them in acidulated water to prevent browning. ○○ serves 4

Juice of 1 lemon	Sea salt and freshly ground white pepper
2 bunches cardoons	2 tablespoons unsalted butter
1 cup heavy cream	2 tablespoons extra-virgin olive oil
1 cup shredded Fontina cheese	Fresh white truffles for garnish (optional)

Fill a bowl with water and add the lemon juice. Trim the cardoons and cut away any brown spots. Using a small, sharp knife, peel away the tough strings running along each stalk. Place each stalk in the lemon water as you finish.

Have ready a bowl of ice water. Bring a large saucepan of salted water to a boil. Drain the cardoons, add to the boiling water, and blanch until tender, 8 to 10 minutes. Drain and quickly plunge into the ice water. Let cool, then drain again and cut crosswise into 1- or 2-inch pieces. Set aside.

In a saucepan, heat the cream over low heat. Add the cheese and stir until the cheese is melted and you have a smooth sauce. Season to taste with salt and white pepper. Set aside and keep warm.

In a sauté pan, melt the butter over medium heat. Add the blanched cardoons and sauté until crisp-tender, about 2 minutes.

Divide the cardoons among 4 individual plates and ladle the cheese sauce over the top. Drizzle the extra-virgin olive oil on the plates. Shave truffles, if using, over the plates.

scampi alla griglia all'olio extra virgine di oliva, limone e prezzemolo

BILLY'S LANGOUSTINOS

While on tour in the Midwest, the singer Billy Joel often makes Chicago his home base. During those times, he becomes a regular at Spiaggia. Cooked on the grill, these langoustinos are as simple as they are delicious. We made some this way for Billy one night, and now he orders them every time he dines with us. Though the dish is not on the menu, all the cooks know how to prepare "Billy's Langoustinos." ○ ○ serves 4

24 large langoustinos (see recipe introduction, page 64), about 3 pounds total weight, shells on

¾ cup extra-virgin olive oil

Sea salt and freshly ground pepper

1 teaspoon minced fresh flat-leaf (Italian) parsley

½ cup Lemon Vinaigrette (page 35)

2 cups mâche leaves for garnish (see Notes, page 48)

Prepare a fire in a charcoal grill or preheat a gas grill to 400 degrees F.

Split the langoustinos in half and brush the flesh sides with the olive oil. Season to taste with salt and pepper.

Place the langoustinos, flesh side down, on the hottest part of the grill. Grill until opaque throughout, about 2 minutes.

Stir the parsley into the lemon vinaigrette. Divide the langoustinos among 4 individual plates and drizzle each serving with the dressing. Garnish with mâche leaves and serve immediately.

I PRIMI pasta, risotto, and soup

○ ○ ○ PERHAPS OUR GREATEST COMPLIMENTS COME FROM GUESTS WHO TELL US THAT OUR *PRIMI* MAKE THEM FEEL LIKE THEY ARE DINING IN ITALY. ALTHOUGH IN ITALY PASTA, RISOTTO, AND SOUPS ARE SERVED AS A SEPARATE SMALL-PORTIONED COURSE BETWEEN THE ANTIPASTO AND THE MAIN PLATE, IN MANY ITALIAN RESTAURANTS IN AMERICA *PRIMI* ARE COMMONLY SERVED AS SUBSTANTIAL MAIN COURSES. AT SPIAGGIA, WE STAY TRUE TO THE ITALIAN TRADITION.

PASTA SERVED AT SPIAGGIA IS MADE FRESH DAILY. IN FACT, WE EMPLOY FOUR FULL-TIME PASTA MAKERS WHO CREATE AS MANY AS FIFTEEN DIFFERENT SHAPES EACH DAY. YES, WE LOVE PASTA! MOST OF THE PRIMI ON SPIAGGIA'S MENUS AND IN THIS BOOK ARE MADE WITH FRESH PASTA. SOME OF THE PASTAS IN THE FOLLOWING RECIPES CAN TAKE A LITTLE EXTRA EFFORT TO MAKE. WE SUGGEST HEALTHY-SIZED BATCHES SO YOU'LL HAVE PLENTY OF PASTA ON HAND FOR THE NEXT MEAL. PASTA CAN BE FROZEN, WRAPPED IN PLASTIC, FOR UP TO ONE MONTH.

THE PASTA RECIPES IN THIS CHAPTER ARE JUST A SMALL SAMPLING OF THE MORE THAN THREE HUNDRED VARI-ETIES OF PASTA THAT CAN BE FOUND THROUGHOUT ITALY.

Tips for Making Pasta

○○ Use only type 00 semolina flour (see page 22). It is very easy to work with, and you'll love the texture.

○○ Use only the freshest eggs.

○○ Have ample work space.

○○ Reserve any leftover pasta for another use.

Tips for Making Risotto

○○ Use a heavy-bottomed pan to avoid scorching. This also helps to distribute the heat evenly during cooking.

○○ Use only a wine you would drink when cooking risotto. Pour a glass to use for the rice (and one for you to sip while stirring).

○○ Keep the pot of stock you're using hot on the stove. Add more liquid to the risotto only when the previous liquid has been absorbed. Never drown the risotto with too much liquid, and never let it come to a roiling boil.

○○ Risotto should take only 20 to 25 minutes to prepare, be firm to the bite, and be served and enjoyed immediately.

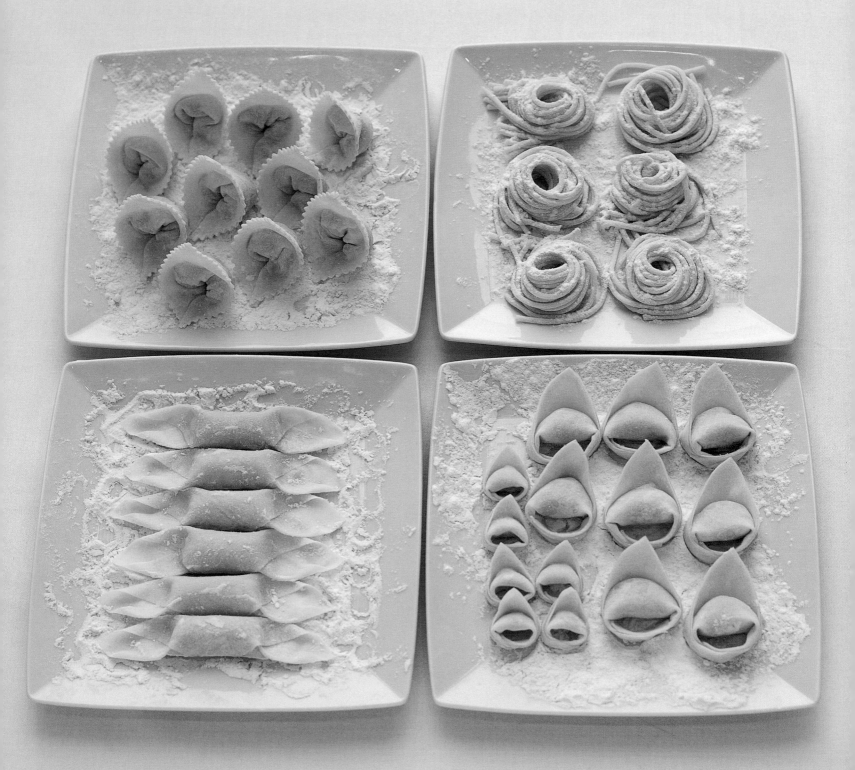

Making Pasta Using the Tools of Antiquity

Before the invention of modern pasta machines and factory-made pasta products, pasta was made at home using a variety of hand tools. To make pasta this old-fashioned way now requires a bit more time, but the texture of the pasta these tools produce is unlike any other fresh or dried pasta you have ever eaten. These pastas are extremely hearty yet impressive, full of hand-crafted appeal. Discussed below are three hand tools used at Spiaggia to create traditional pasta served in a modern style. Like anything worth searching out, these historic devices aren't found just anywhere. Most are not expensive, however, and can be purchased through specialty companies. See Resources (page 186) for information on purchasing these special tools.

the bigolaro

Bigoli is made with a *torchio,* or press, called the *bigolaro*. The *bigolaro* makes long, hollow-tube macaroni similar to *bucatini* or *perciatelli*. In autumn, we serve *bigoli alle castagne in salsa di porcini* (page 90).

The *bigolaro* is an extruder pasta machine. It has a 4-inch-diameter tube at the top that holds the pasta dough. The tube has interchangeable inserts that cut different sizes and thicknesses of *bigoli*. Traditionally, the press is clamped to one end of a small bench and the operator who turns the handles on the press sits at the other end. The pasta dough goes into the tube, and the cranking forces the pasta out through the insert. Once the dough is extruded, the pasta is cut to the desired length, typically about as long as spaghetti. The rough texture of the pasta is what makes *bigoli* so special, as it allows the sauce to cling to it more easily than smooth pastas. There is no substitution for *bigoli;* it is unique.

the chitarra Popular throughout Italy, *pasta alla chitarra* comes from the central regions of Abruzzo and Molise. The simple and ingenious device used to make this pasta is essentially a rectangular beechwood frame over which fine metal strings are stretched at millimeter intervals. A special key is provided to tighten the strings if they become loose over time. The *chitarra* also includes a collecting tray to catch the cut pasta.

To make *pasta alla chitarra,* lay a thinly rolled sheet of dough over the strings of the *chitarra.* Roll a rolling pin over the dough so the metal wires cut it into thin pasta. The resulting pasta has a square-shaped slice, whereas standard spaghetti is round. At Spiaggia you can sample *spaghetti alla chitarra* with red shrimp and baby zucchini (see page 89), or with wild mushrooms and fava beans.

the corzetti stamp These hand-carved wooden pasta stamps are used to make the classic Genoese pasta known as *corzetti*. These "coins" of pasta are so named for the cross designs traditionally carved into the stamps of Genoese nobility.

Modern *corzetti* stamps typically bear flower and nautical designs. The stamps have carvings on both the top and the bottom press. The top of the stamp fits comfortably in your hand, while the bottom of the stamp has one side with a cutting edge for making the dough into disks and one side that imprints the bottom of the pasta disks during stamping. *Corzetti* stamps are not readily available, but are worth the effort to find. They come in great designs and are easy to keep clean.

To make *corzetti,* dust the stamp's base lightly with flour and cut out a round disk from thinly rolled pasta dough. Place the pasta disk on the lightly floured carved end of the stamp base (turn the base over from the cutting side) and press the top of the stamp firmly onto the pasta disk to make the imprint on the dough. Set aside on a lightly floured baking sheet and repeat with the remaining dough.

corzetti con polpa di granchio, pancetta, rucola e pomodorini

HAND-STAMPED PASTA DISKS WITH CRAB, PANCETTA, ARUGULA, AND CHERRY TOMATOES

Traditionally, *corzetti* are served with Ligurian Pesto (see page 38), but *corzetti* lend themselves to a variety of sauces. ○ ○ serves 4 with leftovers

½ recipe Basic Pasta Dough (page 44)

3 ounces pancetta, finely diced

2 cups Chicken Stock (page 32) or prepared broth

8 ounces fresh lump crabmeat, picked over for shell fragments

½ cup cherry tomatoes, sliced

Sea salt and freshly ground pepper

2 cups loosely packed fresh arugula leaves

Roll out the pasta dough into thin sheets as directed in the Note on page 44. Make *corzetti* pasta disks as directed on page 85.

Bring a large pot of lightly salted water to a boil.

Meanwhile, place the pancetta in a sauté pan over medium-high heat. Sauté until crispy, 4 to 5 minutes. Pour off the excess fat and add the stock, scraping the browned bits off the bottom of the pan. Bring to a simmer and cook until the liquid is reduced by half, 10 to 12 minutes. Reduce the heat to medium, add the crabmeat and tomatoes, and cook just until heated through. Season with salt and pepper to taste. Keep the sauce warm over very low heat.

Add 32 *corzetti* to the pot of water and cook for 3 to 4 minutes after they rise to the surface. The pasta should be firm to the touch. Add the *corzetti* to the sauce. Cook for 2 minutes over very low heat to allow the pasta to marry with the sauce.

Divide the *corzetti* among 4 warmed plates. Garnish with the arugula and serve immediately.

notes ○ ○ If you like, use a full recipe of Basic Pasta Dough and freeze the extra *corzetti*. Place on a baking sheet lined with parchment paper and dusted with flour and freeze for 10 minutes, or until hard. Transfer to zippered plastic bags and freeze for up to 1 month. Cook in boiling water directly from the freezer. ○ ○ You may substitute vegetable stock or broth for the chicken stock.

spaghetti alla chitarra con gamberoni rossi e zucchine

"GUITAR STRING" PASTA WITH RED SHRIMP AND BABY ZUCCHINI

Although shellfish and zucchini taste great together anytime, we feature this dish in the springtime when baby zucchini are particularly flavorful. The vibrant red shrimp and bright green zucchini give this dish a profoundly Italian look. You can substitute 8 ounces dried spaghetti in this recipe. Lobster stock can be purchased at your local seafood store. See page 85 for information about the *chitarra* pasta tool. ○○ serves 4

½ recipe Basic Pasta Dough (page 44)

2 tablespoons extra-virgin olive oil

2 cloves garlic

8 large red shrimp (see recipe introduction), heads on, shelled and deveined, or 1 pound medium to large shrimp, shelled and deveined

½ cup thinly sliced baby zucchini

2 cups lobster stock (see recipe introduction)

Sea salt and freshly ground pepper

¼ cup unsalted butter, cut into small pieces

4 fresh basil leaves

Roll out the pasta dough into thin sheets as directed on page 44. Cut the pasta dough into "guitar string" pasta using a *chitarra* as directed on page 85. Place the pasta on a lightly floured board or cloth as it's finished.

Bring a large pot of lightly salted water to a boil. Add the pasta and cook until al dente (tender but firm to the bite), 5 to 7 minutes.

Meanwhile, in a large saucepan over medium-high heat, heat the olive oil. Add the garlic and cook until lightly browned, about 1 minute. Add the shrimp and cook until lightly browned on one side, about 2 minutes. Turn the shrimp over and add the zucchini and lobster stock; cook until the sauce thickens, 2 to 3 minutes. Season with salt and pepper to taste. Set aside and keep warm.

Drain the pasta. Immediately add the pasta to the saucepan. Cook over low heat for about 2 minutes to allow the pasta to marry with the sauce. The pasta should still be firm to the bite. Remove from the heat and toss in the butter until melted.

Divide among 4 warmed plates. Garnish each serving with a basil leaf and serve immediately.

bigoli alle castagne in salsa di porcini

HANDMADE PASTA TUBES WITH PORCINI MUSHROOM SAUCE

To make pasta this old-fashioned way requires time and patience, but the texture of *bigoli* is unlike any other fresh or dried pasta. Chestnut *bigoli* is extremely satisfying and hearty, but with an impressive gourmet flair. This traditional thick pasta yields healthy-sized servings. For a fun presentation, curl about a ½-cup serving of *bigoli* around a large fork for plating. For more information on *bigoli* and the machine that makes it, see page 84. If you do not have a *bigolaro,* you can substitute tagliatelle, as directed on page 92. o ○

For the Chestnut Pasta Dough:

1 cup type 00 semolina flour (see page 22)

1 cup chestnut flour (see Notes)

1 teaspoon sea salt

8 egg yolks, lightly beaten

2 to 3 tablespoons water

4 tablespoons unsalted butter

4 ounces dried porcini mushrooms, reconstituted and thinly sliced (see page 24)

8 ounces fresh porcini or cremini mushrooms, brushed clean and sliced

4 cups Veal Stock (page 33)

3 cloves garlic, minced

1 cup dry white wine

1 teaspoon tomato paste

2 sprigs fresh rosemary

¼ cup grated Parmigiano-Reggiano or Parmesan cheese, plus extra for serving

½ cup mixed microgreens for garnish (see Notes)

2 tablespoons diced fresh tomato for garnish

To make the pasta dough. Sift the flours and salt into a bowl, then mound onto a pastry board or other wood or plastic work surface. Make a well in the center and add the egg yolks. Using a fork, gradually fold the flour into the eggs, adding the water little by little until you have a soft dough. Knead a few times until smooth, then form the dough into a ball, wrap in plastic, and refrigerate for 1 hour.

In a large saucepan over medium-high heat, melt 2 tablespoons of the butter. Add all of the mushrooms and sauté until lightly browned, about 8 minutes. Transfer to a bowl.

In a small saucepan, heat the stock. Return the saucepan used to cook the mushrooms to medium-high heat. Add the garlic and sauté for 1 minute. Add the wine and bring to a

continued o ○

simmer, scraping the browned bits off the bottom of the pan. Cook until the liquid is reduced by half, about 10 minutes. Stir in the tomato paste. Add the hot stock, mushrooms, and rosemary sprigs. Reduce the heat to medium and cook until the liquid is reduced by half, 45 to 60 minutes. Discard the rosemary sprigs and keep the sauce warm.

Meanwhile, make the *bigoli* as directed on page 84. Or, roll the dough and cut the pasta into ⅛-inch ribbons for tagliatelle. Place the pasta on a lightly floured board or cloth as it's finished and let dry for 5 minutes. Measure out three-fourths of the pasta; reserve the remainder for another use.

Bring a large pot of lightly salted water to a boil. Add three-fourths of the pasta and cook until al dente (tender but firm to the bite), about 2 minutes.

Drain the pasta and return to the pot. Add the sauce to the pot and stir to combine. Cook over low heat for about 2 minutes to allow the pasta to marry with the sauce. Stir in the remaining 2 tablespoons butter and the ¼ cup Parmigiano-Reggiano.

To serve, divide among warmed plates. Sprinkle with Parmigiano-Reggiano. Garnish with microgreens and tomatoes and serve immediately.

notes o○ Chestnut flour can be found at Italian markets, natural foods stores, and well-stocked supermarkets. o○ See Resources (page 186) for information on purchasing microgreens.

gnocchi di patate con coniglio brasato

POTATO PASTA DUMPLINGS WITH BRAISED RABBIT

The potato gnocchi of southern Italy have a flavor and texture that make them unique among pastas. Gnocchi are popular and virtually irresistible, and very versatile because they go well with many different sauces. This recipe with braised rabbit is a traditional family favorite.

○ ○ serves 8 with leftovers

1 rabbit, about 3 pounds, cut into 8 serving pieces (see Notes)

Sea salt and freshly ground black pepper

5 tablespoons extra-virgin olive oil

2 yellow onions, coarsely chopped

2 cloves garlic, crushed

2 cups dry white wine

1 cup canned Italian plum tomatoes, preferably San Marzano, with their juices

8 cups Chicken Stock (page 32) or prepared broth

4 sprigs fresh thyme

1 large sprig fresh rosemary

Grated Parmigiano-Reggiano or Parmesan cheese, for serving

For the Potato Gnocchi:

2 russet potatoes, about 1 pound total weight

2 egg yolks

Salt and freshly ground white pepper

2 cups unbleached all-purpose flour

Preheat the oven to 350 degrees F.

Season the rabbit pieces generously with salt and black pepper. In a large, deep ovenproof skillet or Dutch oven over medium-high heat, heat 3 tablespoons of the olive oil. Add the rabbit in 2 batches and brown on both sides, turning once, about 6 minutes per batch. As each piece is browned, transfer to a plate.

When all of the rabbit is browned, reduce the heat to medium and heat the remaining 2 tablespoons olive oil in the same pan. Add the onions and garlic and cook, stirring frequently, until the onions are beginning to brown, 4 to 5 minutes. Add the wine and bring to a simmer, scraping the browned bits off the bottom of the pan. Cook until the wine is reduced by half, about 5 minutes. Stir in the tomatoes, stock, thyme, and rosemary. Nestle the rabbit pieces in the sauce and return to a simmer.

continued ○ ○

Cover the skillet tightly with a lid or heavy-duty aluminum foil, transfer to the oven, and braise for 30 minutes. Turn the pieces over and continue to braise, covered, until the rabbit is tender, 25 to 30 minutes longer.

While the rabbit is braising, make the gnocchi: Wash and prick the potatoes with a fork. Bake the potatoes in the oven, with the rabbit, until tender when pierced with a fork, about 1 hour. While they are still hot, peel the potatoes and pass them through a potato ricer into a bowl, or mash by hand in the bowl with a potato masher. Working as quickly as possible, add the egg yolks and a generous pinch of salt and white pepper. Lightly toss the eggs with the potatoes and fold in the flour until combined with the potato in a smooth dough. (A pastry cutter is helpful here; kneading the dough can make the gnocchi doughy and heavy.) Pull off 4-inch-sized pieces of the dough and roll into ropes about ½ inch thick. Cut the ropes into 1-inch-long dumplings. Roll each dumpling gently in the palm of your hand, first into a ball and then, with your thumb, taper the ends to resemble a football. Arrange the finished gnocchi, not touching, on a lightly floured board or cloth and let dry for 15 minutes.

Using tongs, transfer the rabbit pieces to a platter. Discard the herb sprigs from the sauce. Strain the sauce into a bowl through a fine-mesh sieve and return to the pan. Simmer over medium-high heat until the sauce is thickened and coats the back of a spoon, 20 to 30 minutes. Taste and adjust the seasoning.

While the sauce is reducing, remove the rabbit meat from the bones. Discard the bones and skin. Return the rabbit to the reduced sauce and keep warm until ready to serve.

To cook the gnocchi, bring a large pot of lightly salted water to a boil. Add the gnocchi and cook for 3 minutes after they rise to the surface. Drain the gnocchi and add to the pan with the rabbit and the sauce. Place over low heat for 1 to 2 minutes to allow the gnocchi to marry with the meat and sauce. Taste and adjust the seasoning. Divide the rabbit and pasta among warmed individual plates and spoon more sauce over. Serve immediately, passing the Parmigiano-Reggiano at the table.

notes o○ The rabbit can be braised in the sauce 1 day ahead and refrigerated. Reheat slowly on the stove top until warmed through. o○ Gnocchi can be made in advance and frozen. Place them, not touching, on a baking sheet lined with parchment paper and dusted with flour and freeze for 20 minutes or until hard. Transfer to zippered plastic bags and freeze for up to 1 month. Cook in boiling water directly from the freezer.

tagliatelle ai tartufi bianchi

HOMEMADE PASTA RIBBONS WITH WHITE TRUFFLES

This is the best way to enjoy fresh white truffles, the Piemontese way! o ○ serves 4

½ recipe Basic Pasta Dough (see page 44)

2 cups Chicken Stock (see page 32)

½ cup unsalted butter

½ cup grated Parmigiano-Reggiano or Parmesan cheese

2 teaspoons white truffle oil

Fresh white truffle for grating

To make the tagliatelle, roll out the pasta dough into thin sheets as directed on page 44. Using a pasta cutting attachment, cut the pasta into ⅛-inch ribbons. Place the pasta on a lightly floured board or cloth until needed.

In a large saucepan over medium-high heat, heat the chicken stock until it comes to a boil. Reduce heat to medium-low and add the butter, stirring until melted. Set aside and keep warm.

Bring a large pot of lightly salted water to a boil. Add the pasta and cook until al dente (tender but firm to the bite), 2 to 3 minutes.

Drain the pasta and add it to the sauce. Cook over low heat for 2 minutes to allow the pasta to marry with the sauce. Remove from the heat and fold in ¼ cup of the Parmigiano-Reggiano and the truffle oil.

Divide the pasta among 4 warmed plates. Sprinkle with the remaining Parmigiano-Reggiano and shave a little of the truffle over each. Serve immediately.

fagottini all'aragosta con dragoncello

"HOBO SACK" PASTA WITH LOBSTER AND LOBSTER TARRAGON SAUCE

These pasta bundles boast a filling of luscious fresh Maine lobster. You can assemble and cook the *fagottini* 1 day in advance, then reheat gently when ready to serve. Note that the lobster shells yield more delectable sauce than we need here; reserve the rest for another use, covered and refrigerated for up to 5 days, or frozen for up to 1 month. ○ ○ serves 4 with leftovers

2 live Maine lobsters, about 1¼ pounds each

¼ cup extra-virgin olive oil

Sea salt and freshly ground pepper

For the Lobster Sauce:

2 tablespoons extra-virgin olive oil

Shells of 2 lobsters (above)

½ yellow onion, finely diced

2 cloves garlic, thinly sliced

1 carrot, peeled and finely diced

1 stalk celery, finely diced

½ teaspoon sea salt

1 tablespoon tomato paste

2 tablespoons brandy

1 cup dry white wine

3 cups water

Basic Pasta Dough (page 44)

8 long, thin fresh chives, blanched for 30 seconds in boiling water

2½ cups Seafood Poaching Liquid (page 36)

2 tablespoons Tarragon Oil (page 37)

Cook, clean, and shell the lobsters as directed for the lobster salad recipe on page 50. Reserve the shells.

In a bowl, toss the tail meat with the ¼ cup olive oil and season with salt and pepper to taste. Refrigerate the lobster meat and the claws until ready to use.

To make the sauce: Heat the 2 tablespoons olive oil in a large saucepan over medium heat. Break the shells into small pieces and add to the pan. Sauté the shells for about 5 minutes. Add the onion, garlic, carrot, celery, and salt and cook until the vegetables are caramelized, 15 to 20 minutes. Add the tomato paste and stir well to combine. Add the brandy and wine and stir to scrape up the browned bits from the bottom of the pan. Add the water and bring to a simmer over medium-high heat. Reduce the heat to

continued ○ ○

medium-low and cook until the sauce is reduced by half, about 1 hour. Remove from the heat and strain through a fine-mesh sieve into a clean saucepan. Set aside.

Bring a large pot of lightly salted water to a boil. Roll out the pasta dough into 2 thin sheets as directed on page 44. Using a chef's knife or pastry wheel, cut each sheet into two 6-inch squares. (Reserve the extra pasta for another use.) Place the squares on a lightly floured board or cloth and let dry for 5 minutes. Have ready a bowl of ice water. Drop the pasta squares into the boiling water and cook for 30 seconds. Carefully remove the pasta sheets with a slotted spoon, shaking to remove excess moisture, and transfer to the ice water to stop the cooking. Working quickly, remove the pasta sheets from the ice water one at a time and lay flat on a cloth to dry. Do not overlap or the squares will stick together.

Prepare the poaching liquid.

Preheat the oven to 350 degrees F. Spread the parboiled pasta squares on a clean, lightly floured work surface. Divide the seasoned lobster tail meat among them, mounding it in the center. Draw up the edges of the pasta squares around the lobster meat and, using 2 chives for each, secure by tying the squares into attractive bundles.

Arrange the lobster bundles in a nonstick roasting pan and pour in the poaching liquid. Lightly oil a sheet of aluminum foil and cover the pan with the foil, oiled side down. Bake until the pasta is tender and the lobster is heated through, 15 to 20 minutes. Remove from the oven and add the lobster claws to the poaching liquid to warm through.

Gently reheat the lobster sauce.

To serve, ladle about ¼ cup of the lobster sauce onto each of 4 warmed plates. Carefully remove the lobster bundles from the roasting pan and place each on the sauce. Place a whole lobster claw next to the pasta. Garnish the plates with the tarragon oil and serve immediately.

agnolotti di vitello con polline di finocchio

VEAL-FILLED CRESCENT RAVIOLI WITH CRISPY VEAL BREAST AND FENNEL POLLEN

Veal breast is a hearty, old-world product. Stuffed with crusty bread, herbs, and garlic, veal roast is perfect for Sunday dinners and family holidays, but we wanted a more elegant version of this dish for Spiaggia. We finally decided to incorporate them into the cresent-shaped ravioli called *agnolotti*. The filling is the meat from around the bones; the top cap of the roast is removed and crisped like bacon and then sprinkled over the top of the *agnolotti*. Finally, a sprinkling of fennel pollen adds another layer of flavor and also cuts the richness of this flavorful meat. The veal breast takes 10 to 12 hours to cook, so we recommend cooking it 1 day ahead of serving. These stuffed *agnolotti* will satisfy hearty appetites! o o serves 6 to 8

1 whole bone-in veal breast, about 3 pounds

Sea salt and freshly ground pepper

2 tablespoons extra-virgin olive oil

½ recipe Basic Pasta Dough (page 44)

1 cup dried bread crumbs, or as needed

1 egg

1½ cups grated Parmigiano-Reggiano or Parmesan cheese, plus more if needed

4 cups Veal Sauce (page 39)

½ teaspoon fennel pollen (see Notes)

4 sprigs fennel fronds (optional)

Preheat the oven to 200 degrees F.

Season the veal breast with salt and pepper. Place on a rack in a roasting pan and roast until browned and falling-apart tender, 10 to 12 hours. Remove from the pan and pat dry. Separate the top cap from the meat and pull the meat from the bones.

Raise the oven temperature to 375 degrees F. Julienne ½ cup of the top cap and place in a baking pan. Drizzle with the olive oil and bake until the meat is browned and crispy, about 1 hour. Transfer to paper towels to drain.

Meanwhile, roll out the pasta dough into thin sheets as directed on page 44. Let the pasta sheets rest on a lightly floured work surface or cloths while you make the filling.

In a food processor, grind the remaining veal meat. Add the 1 cup bread crumbs, the egg, and ½ cup of the Parmigiano-Reggiano and pulse to combine. The filling should not be wet; add more bread crumbs and/or cheese if necessary. Taste and adjust the seasoning.
continued o o

In a large sauté pan over medium heat, gently reheat the veal sauce and keep warm.

Cut the pasta sheets into 3-inch squares. To fill, place a dough square in front of you on the diagonal, so you are facing a diamond shape. Place a teaspoon of filling in the middle of the diamond. Lightly spray the pasta with water and bring the bottom point of the diamond up to the top point. Press the pasta together to form a triangle, working out from the filling. Roll the folded edge of the triangle up once, and then once again, flipping the pasta over. Gently press the edges of the pasta to seal in the filling. Repeat with the remaining dough and filling. Arrange the finished *agnolotti* on a lightly floured board or cloth so that they are not touching and let dry for 5 minutes.

When all the *agnolotti* are assembled, bring a large pot of lightly salted water to a boil. Add the *agnolotti* to the boiling water and cook until al dente (tender but firm to the bite), 2 to 3 minutes after they rise to the top. Remove with a slotted spoon and carefully transfer to the pan of veal sauce. Gently toss the *agnolotti* with the sauce over low heat for 2 minutes to allow them to marry with the sauce and absorb some of it. The pasta should still be firm to the bite.

To serve, place about 1 tablespoon of the Parmigiano-Reggiano on each warmed individual plate. Divide the *agnolotti* among the plates, arranging them on top of the cheese. Sprinkle another 1 tablespoon of the cheese over the pasta and crumble the crispy veal breast on top. Garnish each plate with fennel pollen and fennel fronds, if using. Serve immediately.

notes o○ *Agnolotti* can be assembled in advance and frozen. Line a baking sheet with parchment paper and dust with flour. Arrange them, not touching, on the sheet. Freeze until hard, about 20 minutes. Transfer to zippered plastic bags and freeze for up to 1 month. o○ Fennel pollen comes from wild fennel plants found in California. The tiny yellow flowers from the plants are collected when in full bloom. They are then dried and the pollen is harvested. Fennel pollen has the intense essence of fennel flavor. Use it sparingly to season dishes just before serving.

ravioletti di crescenza con salsa di parmigiano-reggiano e burro al tartufo

CRESCENZA RAVIOLI WITH PARMIGIANO-REGGIANO AND TRUFFLE BUTTER SAUCE

Elegant and rich, this pasta dish is all about top-quality ingredients. Crescenza cheese is a soft, fresh creamy cheese that is ideal for these pasta pillows. ○○ serves 12

Basic Pasta Dough (page 44)

1 pound Crescenza cheese

½ stick cold butter, plus 1½ cups unsalted butter

⅓ cup truffle oil

1½ cups grated Parmigiano-Reggiano or Parmesan cheese

12 cloves garlic, thinly sliced, crisped in olive oil

12 small sprigs fresh rosemary

1 cup edible flower petals (optional)

Preheat the oven to 375 degrees F.

Roll out the pasta dough into thin sheets as directed on page 44. Using a chef's knife or pastry wheel, cut the pasta sheets into twenty-four 5-by-5-inch squares. Place the squares on a lightly floured board or cloth until ready to cook. Cut out 24 rectangles of parchment paper, each 7- by 7½-inches. Grease each piece using the cold stick of butter, leaving a 1½-inch border unbuttered.

Have ready a bowl of ice water. Bring a large pot of lightly salted water to a boil. Add the pasta squares to the boiling water and cook until al dente (tender but firm to the bite), 1 to 2 minutes. Remove the pasta squares with a slotted spoon, shaking to remove excess moisture, and transfer carefully to the ice water to stop the cooking. Working quickly, remove the pasta squares from the ice water one at a time, and lay flat on a cloth to dry. Do not overlap, or the squares will stick together.

Cut the Crescenza cheese into 24 pieces, each about 2 inches wide, 2 inches long, and ¼ inch thick. Place a piece of the cheese in the middle of each pasta square and fold the bottom and top flap of pasta over the middle, wrapping it around the cheese. Then fold the sides into the middle, burrito style. Place the *ravioletto,* seam side down, in the middle of a buttered parchment piece and fold the parchment around the pasta, repeating the technique used to wrap the pasta around the cheese. Place the parchment packet, seam side down, on a baking sheet. Repeat with the remaining pasta, cheese, and parchment.

Bake until the edges of the parchment paper are barely golden brown, 10 to 12 minutes.

Meanwhile, in a saucepan over medium heat, melt the 1½ cups butter. Cook to a nutty brown color, 4 to 6 minutes. Stir in the truffle oil.

To serve, place 1 tablespoon of the Parmigiano-Reggiano in the center of each of 12 warmed plates. Carefully remove the parchment around a *ravioletto* and place it on the grated cheese. Arrange a second *ravioletto* next to the first. Spoon 2 tablespoons of the truffle butter over the *ravioletti*. Sprinkle with another 1 tablespoon Parmigiano-Reggiano. Garnish with the garlic crisps, rosemary, and flower petals, if using. Repeat to make the remaining 11 servings. Serve immediately.

note ○○ Wrapped in the parchment and placed in an airtight container, the *ravioletti* freeze well for up to 1 month. Bake right from the freezer for 25 minutes, and continue as directed.

cappellacci di zucca con salvia

PASTA HATS WITH PUMPKIN AND SAGE

This dish may well become a family favorite, especially at Thanksgiving, when pumpkins are in season. The filling has a sweet-and-savory flavor that pairs well with turkey, goose, or duck. Whenever we serve this dish to customers and friends who have never tried it, the raves are loud and clear. This stuffed pasta yields hearty portions, and we suggest serving with a robust red wine. ○○ serves 6 to 8

For the Pumpkin Filling:

1 pie pumpkin, about 2 pounds (about 2 cups purée after roasting)

⅓ cup *mostarda*, coarsely chopped (see Notes)

1¼ cups dried bread crumbs

1¼ cups grated Parmigiano-Reggiano or Parmesan cheese

1 cup amaretti cookies, finely ground

¼ teaspoon freshly grated nutmeg

Sea salt and freshly ground pepper

½ recipe Basic Pasta Dough (page 44)

2 cups unsalted butter

16 fresh sage leaves

Grated Parmigiano-Reggiano or Parmesan cheese, for serving

Preheat the oven to 400 degrees F. To make the filling: Cut the pumpkin in half and remove the seeds. Arrange, cut sides down, on an aluminum foil–lined or nonstick baking sheet and roast until very tender, 20 to 30 minutes. When cool enough to handle, scoop out the flesh and place in a blender or food processor. Add the *mostarda* and process to a purée. Transfer to a bowl and add the bread crumbs, cheese, cookie crumbs, and nutmeg. Stir to combine. Season with salt and pepper to taste. Set aside.

Roll out the pasta dough into thin sheets as directed on page 44. Working with one sheet at a time, cut the pasta into 3-inch squares. Place each square on a lightly floured board or cloth and let dry for 5 minutes.

To fill, place a dough square in front of you on the diagonal, so you are facing a diamond shape. Place a teaspoon of filling in the middle of the diamond. Lightly spray the pasta with water and bring the bottom point of the diamond to the top point. Press the pasta together to form a triangle, working out from the filling. Trim the 2 unfolded sides of

continued ○○

the pasta triangle with a crimped pastry wheel, and then fold the side points of the pasta forward and press to join them together in a "bishop's hat" shape. Repeat with the remaining dough and filling. Stand the finished *cappellacci* to dry for about 5 minutes on a baking sheet lined with parchment paper and dusted with flour.

Bring a large pot of lightly salted water to a boil. Meanwhile, in a large sauté pan, melt the butter over medium heat; do not let the butter brown. Stir in the sage leaves. Set aside and keep warm over very low heat.

Add the *cappellacci* to the boiling water and cook until al dente (tender but firm to the bite), 3 to 5 minutes after they rise to the top. Remove with a slotted spoon and carefully transfer to the warm butter and sage sauce. Cook for 1 to 2 minutes to allow the pasta to marry with the sauce and absorb some of it.

To serve, divide the *cappellacci* among 8 warmed plates and top with Parmigiano-Reggiano. Serve immediately.

notes ○○ *Mostarda* is candied fruit, such as pears, apricots, and cherries, mixed with white mustard and sugar syrup. More sweet than piquant, *mostarda* adds dimension to the pumpkin filling. It is also used with boiled meats and in confections. You can find *mostarda* in Italian specialty stores or on-line, or see the recipe for Spiaggia's Orange and Lemon Mostarda (page 164). See Resources (page 186) for information on purchasing *mostarda*. ○○ The *cappellacci* can be assembled in advance and frozen. Arrange them, not touching, on a baking sheet lined with parchment paper and dusted with flour. Freeze until hard, about 20 minutes. Transfer to zippered plastic bags and freeze for up to 1 month.

risotto con pancetta, peperoni e succo d'uva

RISOTTO WITH MELROSE PEPPERS, BRAISED PORK BELLY, AND VERJUS

Melrose Park, an Italian-American suburb west of Chicago, has many vegetable gardens. A smallish green pepper, known as the Melrose pepper, appears every summer in the local farmers' market, grown in those very gardens. The onions we use for this risotto at Spiaggia are also locally grown; here they are called torpedo onions, but they are the same variety as the famous Tropea onions grown on the Calabrian coast.

You should order fresh pork belly from the butcher two days before needed. Cook the pork belly the day before you make the risotto. When you are ready to serve it, you will need to crisp it in a cast-iron or nonstick frying pan.

Verjus is unfermented grape juice, used mostly as a wine-friendly alternative to vinegar. It can be hard to find; check specialty gourmet stores and see Resources (page 186). ○○ serves 4

8-ounce piece fresh pork belly (see recipe introduction)

2 tablespoons olive oil for roasting

1 cup *verjus* (see recipe introduction)

3 cups Chicken Stock (page 32) or prepared broth

4 tablespoons unsalted butter

½ cup julienned torpedo onion or other sweet onion such as Vidalia or Walla Walla

½ cup julienned Melrose pepper or green bell pepper

¾ cup Carnaroli rice

¼ cup grated Parmigiano-Reggiano or Parmesan cheese

Sea salt and freshly ground pepper

½ cup micro sorrel for garnish (see Note)

Preheat the oven to 275 degrees F.

Place the pork belly in a heavy-duty baking pan and sprinkle with the olive oil. Turn to coat. Roast until falling-apart tender, 6 to 8 hours. Remove from the oven and transfer to paper towels to drain. Cut into 4 equal squares and refrigerate until ready to use.

Put the *verjus* in a saucepan and bring to a simmer over medium heat. Cook until reduced to a syrupy consistency, 20 to 30 minutes. Set aside.

In another saucepan over medium heat, bring the stock to a gentle simmer and maintain over low heat.

continued ○○

In a heavy-bottomed skillet over low heat, melt 2 tablespoons of the butter. Add the onion and pepper and cook, stirring occasionally, until the onion is translucent, about 7 minutes. Increase the heat to medium-high, add the rice, and stir with a wooden spoon, making sure that every grain is well coated with butter.

Stir the hot stock into the skillet a ladleful at a time and let simmer after each addition. Stir continuously with a wooden spoon, waiting until the liquid is almost completely absorbed before adding more stock. When all the liquid has been added and the rice is al dente (tender but firm to the bite), stir in the remaining 2 tablespoons butter and the Parmigiano-Reggiano and remove from the heat. Season with salt and pepper to taste.

Meanwhile, in a cast-iron or nonstick skillet over medium heat, crisp the pork belly squares until well browned, about 7 minutes on each side. Season with salt and pepper to taste. Transfer to paper towels to drain.

Divide the risotto among 4 warmed plates. Place a piece of braised pork belly on top of each serving. Drizzle the *verjus* syrup all around each plate, garnish with micro sorrel leaves, and serve immediately.

note o○ Micro sorrel is a citrusy and slightly sour-tasting sprout that can be found at some specialty produce stores, or see Resources (page 186).

zuppa gran faro

TUSCAN BEAN AND SPELT SOUP

This soup, a traditional Tuscan dish made with spelt, is a specialty of the area around Lucca. Trattoria La Mora in Ponte a Moriano, just outside of Lucca, is a busy restaurant on the road to Abetone, a popular ski town. The Brunicardi family, the owners of the trattoria, warm up many skiers with this incredible hot and hearty fare. Spelt is an ancient cereal grain with a nutty flavor and has a higher protein content than wheat. It can be found in natural foods stores and well-stocked supermarkets. ○○ makes 8 cups

¼ cup olive oil

1 ounce prosciutto, diced

1 ounce pancetta, diced

1 slice bacon, diced

⅓ cup chopped celery

⅓ cup peeled and diced carrot

⅓ cup diced yellow onion

2 cloves garlic, chopped

1¾ cups dried white beans such as cannellini or Great Northern, picked over, rinsed, and soaked in cold water to cover overnight

8 cups Chicken Stock (page 32) or prepared broth

One 16-ounce can Italian plum tomatoes, preferably San Marzano, with their juices, or 16 ounces Italian tomato purée

2 large sprigs fresh rosemary

1 cup spelt (see recipe introduction)

Extra-virgin olive oil for drizzling

Parmigiano-Reggiano shavings or Parmesan cheese for garnish

12 sprigs chervil for garnish

In a large stockpot over medium-low heat, heat the olive oil. Add the prosciutto, pancetta, and bacon and sauté until crisp, 7 to 10 minutes. Add the celery, carrot, onion, and garlic and continue to sauté until slightly caramelized, about 8 minutes. Drain the beans and add to the pot with the stock. Pass the tomatoes through a food mill and add to the pot with the rosemary. Raise the heat to medium-high, bring to a simmer, and then reduce the heat to low and cook until the beans are tender, about 40 minutes. Discard the rosemary.

Meanwhile, put the spelt in a medium saucepan of lightly salted water and bring to a boil over high heat. Reduce heat to medium low and cook until al dente (tender but firm to the bite), about 25 minutes. Drain and set aside.

Purée the soup in small batches in a blender or food processor until smooth and transfer to a heavy saucepan. (The soup should be on the thick side, but can be thinned with more stock or water to the desired consistency.) Reheat gently.

Divide the spelt among warmed individual bowls. Ladle the soup over the spelt and drizzle each serving with the extra-virgin olive oil. Garnish with Parmigiano-Reggiano and chervil. Serve immediately.

note ○○ You can halve this recipe to satisfy lesser appetites. Or, store leftovers in the refrigerator for up to 5 days.

I SECONDI main courses

○ ○ ○ THE SIMPLEST COOKING TECHNIQUES, COMBINED WITH THE BEST RAW MATERIALS, RESULT IN THE MOST SATISFYING DISHES. THIS IS THE ITALIAN SPIRIT OF GOOD COOKING.

THE TECHNIQUE OF LONG ROASTING AND BRAISING AT LOW TEMPERATURES IS AN AGE-OLD WAY TO TENDERIZE TOUGH BUT VERY FLAVORFUL CUTS OF INEXPENSIVE MEAT. THIS PRACTICE WAS THE WAY OF LIFE IN MANY VILLAGES THROUGHOUT OLD ITALY.

AT SPIAGGIA, WE PREFER THE FRESH FLAVORS OF WILD FISH AND NATURALLY RAISED PORK AND LAMB. SINCE OPENING DAY WE HAVE COOKED IN WOOD-BURNING OVENS. FOOD THAT GOES IN COMES OUT CRUSTY, SMOKY, AND FLAVORFUL. A HOME OVEN CAN ACHIEVE EXCELLENT RESULTS AS WELL.

SUBTLE BALANCING OF OLD WORLD HABITS WITH NEW WORLD CARE MAKES SPIAGGIA'S MAIN COURSES SHINE. WE THINK YOU WILL ENJOY THE RESULTS AT YOUR OWN TABLE.

spigola del mediterraneo con finocchio brasato

POACHED MEDITERRANEAN SEA BASS WITH BRAISED FENNEL

Poaching fish is quick, and the assembly for this dish is easy, which makes this a good recipe to serve when entertaining. You can also prepare the fennel ahead of time. ○○ serves 4

For the Braised Fennel:

2 fennel bulbs, stems and any bruised spots trimmed, with a few feathery tops reserved for garnish (see Notes)

½ cup water

¼ cup extra-virgin olive oil

Sea salt and freshly ground pepper

7½ cups Seafood Poaching Liquid (page 36)

8 skin-on sea bass fillets, 3 ounces each

Extra-virgin olive oil for drizzling

Sea salt

12 Taggiasca or Alfonso olives, pitted, for garnish

½ teaspoon fennel pollen (see Notes page 103) for garnish

Preheat the oven to 350 degrees F.

To make the braised fennel: Core the bulbs and cut into slices about ½ inch thick. Cut the slices into strips about 2 inches long and ¼ inch wide. Arrange the fennel in a baking pan, add the water, and drizzle with the olive oil. Season to taste with salt and pepper. Cover the pan tightly with aluminum foil and bake until tender, about 1 hour, checking after 30 minutes. Set aside 4 fennel strips and keep warm. Transfer the remaining fennel to a food processor and purée until smooth and creamy, adding a teaspoon or two of the braising liquid if necessary. Set aside and keep warm. Reserve any remaining braising liquid for serving.

In a deep sauté pan, heat the poaching liquid until hot but not boiling. Arrange the fish fillets in the pan skin side down, in a single layer, and reduce the heat to a bare simmer. Poach the fillets until just opaque throughout, 5 to 8 minutes, depending on the thickness of the fillets.

Meanwhile, gently reheat the puréed fennel, fennel strips, and reserved braising liquid, if necessary.

Spoon some fennel purée onto the center of each of 4 warmed plates. Pool a little braising liquid at the edge of the fennel purée and place a braised fennel strip on top. Using a slotted spoon, carefully remove 2 fish fillets from the poaching liquid and place on top of the fennel purée, skin side down. Drizzle with olive oil, sprinkle with a pinch of salt, and garnish with 3 olives, fennel pollen, and fennel fronds. Repeat to make the remaining 3 servings.

notes ○○ This recipe is best suited to mild-flavored, white-fleshed fish. If sea bass is not available, you can substitute red snapper, halibut, or flounder. ○○ Put the fennel fronds in a bowl of ice water until ready to use to prevent wilting. ○○ Baby fennel may be substituted for the fennel strips. ○○ Dried tomato slices make a colorful, optional garnish for this dish.

filetto di orata al sale marino con funghi di bosco e tartufo nero

GRILLED BREAM WITH WILD MUSHROOMS

A hearty-flavored fish, sea bream is firm enough to stand up to the charcoal grill and flavorful enough to combine with this autumn assortment of mushrooms. A few julienned pieces of black truffle add a touch of class. ○○ serves 4

8 tablespoons unsalted butter

2 to 3 ounces fresh wild mushrooms such as Trumpet Royale, Honshimegi, and Cinnamon Cap or chanterelles, morels, oysters, or porcini, brushed clean and sliced

½ cup dry white wine

½ cup Chicken Stock (page 32) or prepared broth

4 skin-on bream fillets, 6 ounces each

Extra-virgin olive oil for brushing and drizzling

Sea salt and freshly ground pepper

Black Truffle Potato Purée (page 43) for serving

½ ounce julienned fresh black truffle

Small fennel fronds for garnish (optional)

Prepare a fire in a charcoal grill or preheat a gas grill to 400 degrees F.

In a sauté pan over medium heat, melt 2 tablespoons of the butter. Add the mushrooms and sauté until softened and lightly browned, about 4 minutes. Add the wine, scraping the browned bits off the bottom of the pan, and cook to reduce for 2 minutes. Add the stock and cook for another 1 to 2 minutes. Remove from the heat and whisk in the remaining 6 tablespoons butter to thicken the sauce slightly. Set aside.

Brush the fish on both sides with olive oil and season with salt and pepper. Place the fish on the grill, skin side up, and cook for 2 to 3 minutes. Turn the fish over and cook until opaque throughout when tested with the tip of a knife, 2 to 3 minutes longer. Remove from the grill and flip skin side up. Peel away the skin.

To serve, divide the potato purée among the centers of 4 warmed plates. Spoon the mushrooms around the plates, reserving the pan sauce. Place a fish fillet, with the grill marks up, on top of the potatoes and drizzle the butter sauce on top of the fish and around the plates. Drizzle each serving with olive oil and sprinkle with the truffle. Garnish with fennel fronds, if using.

trancio di salmone con verza e pancetta in salsa al marzemino

ROASTED SALMON WITH CABBAGE, PANCETTA, AND MARZEMINO WINE SAUCE

When Henry Bishop III, the sommelier at Spiaggia, is asked why he knows so much about wine, he often answers with, "Because I know nothing about sports." When asked for a red wine that would pair well with cooked salmon, he didn't answer with the expected Pinot Noir. "Marzemino," was Henry's reply. His choice is an excellent match. ○○ serves 4

4 ounces pancetta, cut into ¼-inch cubes, with 4 very slim slices reserved for garnish

4 tablespoons extra-virgin olive oil

4 salmon fillets, 8 ounces each

Sea salt and freshly ground pepper

2 cups julienned green cabbage

1 cup Chicken Stock (page 32) or prepared broth

1 cup Marzemino Wine Sauce (page 40)

Preheat the oven to 400 degrees F. Put the pancetta slices on a nonstick sheet pan. Place another sheet pan on top and bake in the oven until crispy, about 30 minutes. Remove from the oven and carefully drain on paper towels. Set aside.

In a large ovenproof skillet over medium-high heat, heat 2 tablespoons of the olive oil. Season the salmon with salt and pepper and sear in the skillet for 3 to 4 minutes. Flip the salmon over, transfer to the oven, and roast until opaque throughout when tested with the tip of a knife, 3 to 4 minutes (or 6 minutes more for well done). Remove from the oven. Remove the skin.

In a large sauté pan over medium-high, heat the remaining 2 tablespoons olive oil. Add the cubed pancetta and cook until browned and crispy, 3 to 4 minutes. Add the cabbage and sauté until softened, 2 to 3 minutes. Add the stock, bring to a boil, and cook until the liquid is reduced to about ¼ cup, 5 to 7 minutes. Season with salt and pepper to taste.

Meanwhile, reheat the wine sauce over low heat.

To serve, place a lightly oiled ring mold 2 inches wide and 1 inch tall in the center of one of 4 plates. Fill the mold with one-fourth of the cabbage mixture, pressing down gently to pack the layer. Carefully remove the ring mold and place a salmon fillet on top of the cabbage. Repeat to make the remaining 3 servings. Pool each serving with ¼ cup wine sauce and put a pancetta slice alongside the salmon. Serve immediately.

triglia con cuscus trapanese in salsa al marzemino

RED MULLET WITH TRAPANI-STYLE COUSCOUS AND MARZEMINO WINE SAUCE

Red mullet, native to the Mediterranean, is not well known in America but is held in high esteem in Europe. Here, it is served with couscous, a specialty of Trapani, a Sicilian port that faces Morocco, where couscous is a staple. The Trapanese version includes the very Italian ingredients of capers, bell peppers, olives, and sun-dried tomatoes. ○○ serves 4

For the Couscous:

¾ cup couscous

1 cup boiling water

2 tablespoons extra-virgin olive oil

2 tablespoons chopped pitted green olives

2 tablespoons capers, rinsed, drained, and chopped

2 tablespoons finely diced oil-packed sun-dried tomato

2 tablespoons finely diced red bell pepper

Juice of 1 lemon

Sea salt and freshly ground pepper

5 cups Seafood Poaching Liquid (page 36)

8 small whole red mullets, filleted and skinned (see Note)

Sea salt and freshly ground pepper

1 cup Marzemino Wine Sauce (page 40)

To make the couscous: Put the couscous in a heatproof bowl and pour in the boiling water. Cover with plastic wrap and let steam until the water is completely absorbed and the couscous is tender, about 3 minutes. Add the olive oil, olives, capers, tomato, bell pepper, and lemon juice and toss to combine. Season to taste with salt and pepper. Set aside.

In a deep sauté pan, bring the poaching liquid to a boil, then turn off the heat. Season the fish fillets with salt and pepper and add to the hot poaching liquid. Let stand in the liquid until opaque throughout, 2 to 3 minutes. Transfer to a plate with a slotted spoon. Meanwhile, gently reheat the wine sauce.

To serve, mound some of the couscous on each of 4 warmed plates. Arrange 2 fillets on each mound of couscous. Drizzle some wine sauce over the fish and on the plate.

note ○○ See Resources (page 186) for information on purchasing red mullets.

tagliata di tonno con fagioli bianchi e broccoli

GRILLED SLICED TUNA WITH GIANT WHITE BEANS AND ROMANESCO

Tagliata is typically made with steak, or *bistecca,* in Italy, with the name indicating the meat is sliced. It is then dressed with olive oil, rosemary, salt, and pepper and garnished with white beans. These flavors of Tuscany work as well with tuna as they do with *bistecca. Romanesco* is a vegetable with a color similar to broccoli and delicious flavor similar to cauliflower. ○○ serves 4

1 cup dried Peruvian lima beans (see Note), picked over, rinsed, and soaked in cold water to cover overnight

1½ cups extra-virgin olive oil, plus extra for brushing and drizzling

4 sprigs fresh rosemary, with 1 sprig reserved for garnish

Sea salt and freshly ground pepper

1 medium head *romanesco* or 1 small head cauliflower

1 cup Veal Sauce (page 39)

4 fresh tuna steaks, 7 ounces each

Drain the beans and place in a saucepan with water to cover by 3 inches. Bring to a simmer over high heat, then reduce the heat to low and simmer until tender, 1 to 1½ hours. Drain, transfer to a saucepan, and stir in the 1½ cups oil, the rosemary, and salt and pepper to taste. Keep warm. When the beans are almost done, prepare a fire in a charcoal grill or preheat a gas grill to 400 degrees F.

Bring a saucepan of lightly salted water to a boil. Trim the *romanesco* and separate into florets. Discard the stems. Add the *romanesco* florets and cook just until tender, 5 to 7 minutes. Drain. Set aside and keep warm.

Gently reheat the veal sauce. Set aside and keep warm.

Brush the tuna with olive oil and season with salt and pepper. Arrange on the grill and cook, turning once, until rare, 1 to 2 minutes on each side, or until an instant-read thermometer inserted into the thickest part registers 110 degrees F. Cut into ½-inch-thick slices.

To serve, ladle ¼ cup veal sauce onto each of 4 warmed plates. Place about ¼ cup of beans on one side. Arrange the tuna slices on the beans. Add the *romanesco* to each plate. Drizzle the tuna with additional olive oil, sprinkle with salt and pepper, and garnish with a little rosemary. Serve immediately.

note ○○ See Resources (page 186) for information on purchasing Peruvian lima beans.

sogliola con carciofini, pomodori e basilico al vermentino

POACHED DOVER SOLE WITH BABY ARTICHOKES, TOMATOES, BASIL,
AND VERMENTINO WHITE WINE

Dover sole, a favorite fish at Spiaggia, is a mild but elegant fish that lends itself to a variety of preparations and sauces. Commonly seen on menus in Europe, Dover sole seems to be making a comeback in fine dining restaurants in this country as well.

Vermentino is a Ligurian white wine made from grapes of the same name. It has pleasant fruit and bright acidity, making it an ideal wine with delicate fish. Vermentino also has an affinity with artichokes, a vegetable that can be difficult to pair with wine. This recipe was inspired by a dish from the Ligurian coast. ○○ serves 4

2 lemons

12 baby artichokes

4 to 5 large plum (Roma) tomatoes

3 tablespoons olive oil

2 cups Vermentino wine

2 cups Chicken Stock (page 32) or prepared broth

Sea salt and freshly ground pepper

4 fresh whole basil leaves

¼ cup unsalted butter

2½ cups Seafood Poaching Liquid (page 36)

4 Dover sole fillets, 5 ounces each

2 tablespoons Basil Oil (page 37)

1 cup microbasil for garnish (see Note)

Bring a large saucepan of water to a boil.

Meanwhile, fill a large bowl with cold water. Cut one of the lemons in half and squeeze the juice into the bowl, then add the cut lemon halves. Cut off the stem and one-fourth of 1 artichoke. Bend back and snap off the dark green outer leaves at the base until only the pale green and yellow leaves remain. Cut the artichoke in half lengthwise. Using the point of a knife, remove any purple-tipped leaves or fuzzy choke from the center, if necessary. Place the artichoke halves in the lemon water. Repeat with the remaining artichokes.

Squeeze the juice of the remaining lemon into the boiling water. Drain the artichokes and add to the pan. Blanch for 1 minute. Drain and set aside.

Have ready a bowl of ice water. Bring a saucepan of water to a boil over medium-high heat. Core the top and score an X at the bottom (blossom end) of each tomato. Add to the boiling water and blanch for 10 seconds. Drain and quickly plunge the tomatoes into

continued ○○

the ice water. When cool, drain and peel. Cut in half lengthwise and squeeze out the seeds. Set aside.

In a large sauté pan over medium-high heat, heat the olive oil. Add the artichokes and sauté until golden brown, 2 to 3 minutes. Add the Vermentino wine, scraping up any browned bits off the bottom of the pan. Cook until the liquid is reduced by half, 4 to 5 minutes. Add the stock and cook until reduced by half again. Season to taste with salt and pepper. Add the tomatoes and the basil. Remove from the heat and whisk in the butter.

Bring the poaching liquid to a boil, then turn off the heat. Season the fillets with salt and pepper and add to the hot poaching liquid. Let rest, cooking in the liquid, until opaque throughout, 2 to 4 minutes.

Divide the artichoke mixture among the centers of 4 warmed plates. Using a fish spatula or a slotted spoon, carefully remove the fillets from the poaching liquid and place 1 on top of each serving of vegetables. Drizzle the basil oil around and over the plates, garnish with microbasil, and serve.

note ○ ○ See Resources (page 186) for information on purchasing microbasil.

faraona al forno con salsiccia speziata e polenta bianca

ROAST GUINEA HEN WITH HERB SAUSAGE AND WHITE CORN POLENTA

In English, this small bird is called a guinea hen; in French, it is called *pintade,* in Italian, *faraona.* It is one of the juiciest, most delicious birds you will ever taste—what chicken would taste like if it was always moist and juicy and full of flavor. The herb sausage here is made from the legs and thigh meat of the hens, and requires a bit of effort, but is absolutely worthwhile. ○○ serves 4

For the Sausage:

2 guinea hen leg quarters (legs and thighs), plus 2 guinea hen neck skins (see Notes)

½ teaspoon extra-virgin olive oil, plus ¼ cup

¼ teaspoon minced garlic

2 tablespoons extra-virgin olive oil, plus extra for drizzling

4 guinea hen breast halves

Sea salt and freshly ground pepper

1 cup Veal Sauce (page 39)

2 tablespoons unsalted butter

Leaves from 1 sprig fresh rosemary, finely chopped

3 leaves fresh sage, finely chopped

Sea salt and freshly ground pepper

6 ounces porcini mushrooms, brushed clean (see Notes)

1 cup sliced brussel sprouts, blanched

4 baby fennel, trimmed and blanched

1 cup White Corn Polenta (page 42) for serving

Preheat the oven to 425 degrees F.

To make the sausage: Skin and debone the guinea hen legs and thighs. Put the meat and skin through a meat grinder on a coarse setting. Transfer to a bowl and mix in the ½ teaspoon olive oil, the garlic, rosemary, sage, and a generous pinch each of salt and pepper. In a sauté pan, heat the ¼ cup olive oil and cook a small sample of sausage to taste for seasoning. Adjust the seasoning of the batch accordingly. Separate the meat mixture into 2 equal portions and stuff each into a neck skin. Tie off the ends with kitchen string.

In a large, ovenproof and nonstick sauté pan, heat the 2 tablespoons olive oil over medium heat. Season the breasts with salt and pepper. When the pan and oil are hot,

continued ○○

add the breasts, skin side down, and cook for 5 minutes. Turn the breasts over, transfer to the oven, and bake until opaque throughout and the juices run clear, about 15 minutes.

In a separate ovenproof pan, bake the sausages in the oven with the breasts, until golden, about 5 minutes on each side.

Gently reheat the veal sauce and keep warm.

In a medium sauté pan over medium-high heat, melt the butter. Add the mushrooms and sauté until lightly browned, 8 to 10 minutes. Add the blanched brussel sprouts and baby fennel and just heat through.

To serve, place ¼ cup of polenta in the center of each of 4 warmed plates. Arrange the mushrooms and brussel sprouts around the polenta. Place 1 breast half and one fennel bulb on top of the polenta. Slice off the ends of each sausage and cut the sausage in half. Place half a sausage on top of the breast. Ladle veal sauce around the meat. Drizzle the plate with olive oil. Repeat to make the remaining 3 servings. Serve immediately.

notes ○○ Order guinea hens from a specialty butcher, or see Resources (page 186). You will need 2 for this recipe, with 2 leg quarters left over for another use. ○○ You can substitute any mild, herbed commercial poultry sausage for the *faraona* sausage. ○○ You can substitute wild mushrooms for the porcini mushrooms.

piccione alla rossini

GRILLED SQUAB WITH CELERY ROOT, BLACK TRUFFLE SAUCE, AND FOIE GRAS

Meaty squab stands up nicely to charcoal grilling. The addition of foie gras, a truffle-infused sauce, and spinach studded with raisins and pine nuts turns this dish into an updated version of veal Rossini.
○ ○ serves 4

For the Celery Root Purée:

1 large or 2 small celery roots, peeled, stems and any bruised spots trimmed

¼ cup unsalted butter, at room temperature

1 cup heavy cream, warmed

Sea salt and freshly ground white pepper

¾ cup Veal Sauce (page 39)

4 tablespoons white truffle oil

2 tablespoons black truffle paste

4 whole boneless squab, cut into breasts and leg quarters (legs and thighs)

4 tablespoons extra-virgin olive oil

Sea salt and freshly ground black pepper

8 cups spinach leaves, loosely packed

2 tablespoons pine nuts

2 tablespoons golden raisins, plumped in warm water

6 ounces foie gras, cleaned and soaked (see page 22), then cut into 4 equal pieces

1 small Norcia truffle for garnish (optional)

1 cup fresh pea shoots for garnish (optional)

To make the celery root purée: Place the celery root in a saucepan and add water to cover by 2 inches. Bring to a simmer over medium-high heat and cook until tender, about 15 minutes. Drain and return the celery root to the pan. Place over low heat for 2 to 3 minutes to remove any excess water. Mash until smooth and fold in the butter and cream. Season to taste with salt and white pepper. Set aside and keep warm.

Prepare a fire in a charcoal grill or preheat a gas grill to 400 degrees F.

In a saucepan, combine the veal sauce, truffle oil, and truffle paste and stir to combine. Warm gently and set aside.

Coat the squab with 2 tablespoons of the olive oil and season with salt and black pepper. Arrange on the grill and cook, turning once, until rare when tested with a knife, 2 to 3 minutes on each side. Transfer to a platter, tent with aluminum foil, and let rest.

In a sauté pan over medium-high, heat the remaining 2 tablespoons olive oil. Add the spinach and toss quickly just until slightly wilted. Remove from the heat and stir in the pine nuts and plumped raisins.

Heat a nonstick skillet over high heat. Add the foie gras and sear, turning once, for 30 seconds on each side.

To serve, divide the celery root purée among the centers of 4 warmed plates. Top each with a portion of spinach. Lay 2 squab legs on top of the spinach, and then top with a breast. Crown each tower with foie gras and ladle ¼ cup of the truffle sauce on each plate. Shave truffle over each plate and garnish with pea shoots, if using. Serve immediately.

petto di pernice avvolta in guanciale con arance e mirto

BARDED PARTRIDGE BREAST WITH ORANGES AND MYRTLE

The cuisine of Sardinia is markedly different from that of the rest of Italy. Here you find preparations and raw materials that you just don't see elsewhere in Italian cooking. In this dish, partridge is paired with oranges and myrtle. Sardinian myrtle-berry liqueur intensifies the sweetness. Wrapping the breasts in *guanciale* bastes the white meat of partridge to keep it moist as it cooks. See Resources (page 186), for information on purchasing *guanciale,* myrtle liqueur, and fresh myrtle. Balsamic Reduction (page 36) can be substituted for the myrtle liqueur. ○○ serves 4

1 cup myrtle liqueur (see recipe introduction)

4 partridge breasts

2 ounces *guanciale* (see page 23) or pancetta, thinly sliced

1 ounce caul fat (see page 21)

¼ cup extra-virgin olive oil, plus extra for drizzling

1 small head cauliflower, broken into florets

4 cups milk

Sea salt

1 tablespoon unsalted butter

⅓ cup heavy cream

Freshly ground pepper

12 orange segments

¼ cup Veal Sauce (page 39), warmed

4 sprigs fresh myrtle leaves (optional; see recipe introduction)

Preheat the oven to 350 degrees F.

In a small saucepan over medium heat, bring the liqueur to a boil. Reduce the heat to medium-low and simmer until reduced by half, about 30 minutes. Let cool. Transfer to a small plastic squeeze bottle with a sealable top.

Wrap the breasts in the *guanciale* and then wrap the barded breasts in a 5-inch square of caul fat. Heat the ¼ cup olive oil in a nonstick, ovenproof sauté pan over medium-high heat. Add the breasts and cook until golden brown and crisp, 2 to 3 minutes per side. Transfer to the oven and roast, turning every 5 minutes, until crisp all around, 8 to 12 minutes longer. Remove the breasts from the oven, tent with aluminum foil, and let rest for 3 minutes. Remove the caul fat.

Meanwhile, combine the cauliflower, milk, and a pinch of salt in a saucepan over medium heat. Cover the milk with a piece of parchment or waxed paper and cook until the cauliflower is tender, about 15 minutes. Drain, discarding the cooking liquid, and transfer to a blender or food processor. Process to a purée. Fold in the butter and cream and season to taste with salt and pepper. Set aside and keep warm.

Slice each breast on the diagonal into 3 pieces. To serve, place 3 orange segments, evenly spaced, on each of 4 warmed plates and set a piece of partridge breast at a 45-degree angle next to each one. Spoon a small dot of the cauliflower purée behind each slice. Pool veal sauce in front of each slice, followed by a smaller pool of myrtle syrup next to the sauce. Drizzle olive oil over the meat. Repeat to make the remaining 3 servings. Garnish each serving with myrtle leaves, if using.

polletto al forno con verdure di stagione

ROAST POUSSIN WITH SEASONAL VEGETABLES

For this simple recipe, go to your local farmers' market and pick up the freshest vegetables of the season. Feel free to select any seasonal vegetables you like. Have your butcher quarter the poussins, or young chickens, preferably free range and very fresh. ○○ serves 4

4 baby carrots, peeled

4 baby white carrots, peeled

4 baby sweet onions

4 baby turnips, peeled

4 baby beets, peeled

4 poussins, cut into quarters

6 tablespoons extra-virgin olive oil

Leaves from 2 sprigs fresh rosemary, coarsely chopped

Sea salt and freshly ground pepper

1 lemon, halved, seeds removed

20 sprigs micro broccoli rabe or fresh flat-leaf (Italian) parsley for garnish (see Note)

Preheat the oven to 450 degrees F.

Bring a saucepan of lightly salted water to a boil. Add the carrots and blanch for 1 minute. Using a slotted spoon, transfer to a bowl. Repeat to blanch the onions and turnips, adding each to the bowl with the carrots. Cook the beets the same way, but transfer to a separate small bowl to avoid staining.

In a roasting pan, toss the poussin pieces with 4 tablespoons of the olive oil, the rosemary, and salt and pepper to taste. Roast until opaque throughout and the juices run clear, about 25 minutes.

While the poussins are roasting, heat the remaining 2 tablespoons olive oil in a sauté pan over medium heat. Add the blanched vegetables and sauté until nicely browned, about 15 minutes.

Arrange the poussins and vegetables on a platter. Squeeze both lemon halves over the entire dish and then garnish with the micro broccoli rabe. Serve immediately.

note ○○ See Resources (page 186) for information on purchasing micro broccoli rabe.

filetto di manzo con coda di bue e purea di patate peruviane

FILET MIGNON WITH BRAISED OXTAILS AND PURPLE POTATO PURÉE

This is a pull-out-all-the-stops main course. Two ingredients from different parts of town help each other to achieve greatness. The "rich" ingredient, filet mignon, is tender but discreet in flavor, while the oxtail is incredibly flavorful, but not very elegant. Oxtails are the tail meat of steers. They can be found in well-stocked supermarkets and butcher shops. After braising, the oxtail meat is pulled from around the bones. ○○ serves 4

For the Braised Oxtails:

¼ cup extra-virgin olive oil

2 pounds oxtails

1 yellow onion, chopped

3 carrots, peeled and chopped

3 stalks celery, chopped

1 tablespoon tomato paste

1 tablespoon chopped fresh thyme

1 tablespoon chopped fresh flat-leaf (Italian) parsley

1½ cups dry red wine

2 cups Veal Stock (page 33)

2 cups water

1 ounce caul fat (see page 21), cut into four 5-inch squares

For the Oxtail Sauce:

6 tablespoons extra-virgin olive oil

1 small carrot, finely chopped

½ yellow onion, finely chopped

1 stalk celery, finely chopped

1 teaspoon tomato paste

1 bay leaf

5 peppercorns

½ cup dry red wine

1¼ cups reserved braising liquid, above

4 tablespoons extra-virgin olive oil

4 filets mignons, 5 ounces each

Sea salt and freshly ground pepper

2 cups blanched and chopped broccoli rabe (see page 151)

Purple Potato Purée (page 43) for serving

2 cloves garlic, thinly sliced

To make the braised oxtails: In a large roasting pan over medium-high heat, heat the ¼ cup olive oil. When the pan and oil are hot, add the oxtails and sear, turning as needed to brown on all sides, about 4 minutes per side. Transfer to a large stockpot and set aside.

continued ○○

Add the onion, carrots, and celery to the roasting pan and return to medium-high heat. Sauté until the vegetables are softened, about 5 minutes. Add the tomato paste, thyme, and parsley. Stir well to combine and cook, uncovered, until the vegetables are browned, 6 to 8 minutes longer. Add the wine and scrape to loosen any browned bits from the bottom of the pan.

Add the vegetables and liquid to the stockpot, along with the veal stock and water. Bring to a boil, reduce the heat to low, and gently simmer, uncovered, until the oxtail meat just starts to fall off of the bones, about 3 hours. Transfer the oxtails to a platter and let cool. Pull the meat off the bones and set aside. Strain the braising liquid and reserve. Discard the solids. Line a lightly oiled 3-inch ring mold with 1 caul fat square. Pack ½ cup of the braised oxtail meat into the mold, pressing gently to pack the layer. Fold over the edges of the square. Carefully remove the mold. Repeat with the remaining 3 squares. Set aside.

To make the sauce: In a saucepan, heat the 6 tablespoons olive oil over medium-high heat. Add the carrot, onion, and celery and sauté for 3 minutes. Stir in the tomato paste and cook 2 minutes longer. Add the bay leaf, peppercorns, and wine. Bring to a simmer and reduce for 5 minutes. Add the reserved braising liquid, return to a simmer, and cook until reduced to 1 cup, 15 to 20 minutes. Strain. Taste and adjust the seasoning. Keep warm.

Heat a large sauté pan over medium high heat for 1 minute. Add 2 tablespoons olive oil to the pan and heat. Add the oxtail packets, seam side down, and brown for 4 minutes each side. Remove the packets and pat dry with paper towels. Keep warm.

Heat another large sauté pan over medium-high heat for 1 minute. Add the remaining 2 tablespoons olive oil and heat. Season the filets with salt and pepper, add to the pan, and sear for 4 minutes on each side for medium-rare.

Prepare the broccoli rabe.

To serve, place an oxtail packet in the center of one of 4 warmed plates. Arrange a filet mignon on top of the oxtail, then place a large oval of purple potato purée on top of the filet. Ladle ¼ cup of sauce on the plate. Arrange the broccoli rabe and garlic around the packet. Repeat to make the remaining 3 servings and serve immediately.

note ○○ Garnish this dish with Parmigiano-Reggiano crisps, if you wish.

costoletta di vitello con animelle e cicoria

VEAL CHOP WITH CRISPY SWEETBREADS AND SWISS CHARD TIMBALES

The veal chop used to be the benchmark of any great Italian restaurant in America. Long a signature dish at Spiaggia, our chops become a little classier than the usual preparation with the addition of a Swiss chard timbale and crispy sweetbreads. Grilling the chops also gives them more flavor. ○ ○ serves 4

For the Sweetbreads:

½ yellow onion, cut into chunks

½ carrot, peeled and cut into chunks

½ stalk celery, cut into chunks

4 veal sweetbreads, about 2 ounces each, blanched, cleaned, and trimmed

2 cups water

1½ cups dry white wine

¼ cup sea salt

1 pound Swiss chard

6 tablespoons extra-virgin olive oil, plus extra for brushing

Sea salt and freshly ground pepper

1 cup Veal Sauce (page 39)

4 large veal rib chops

Preheat the oven to 375 degrees F. Prepare a fire in a charcoal grill or preheat a gas grill to 400 degrees F.

To make the sweetbreads: Combine the onion, carrot, celery, sweetbreads, water, wine, and salt in a saucepan over medium-high heat. Bring to a simmer, reduce the heat to low, and cook until the sweetbreads are still somewhat firm but silky inside, 3 to 5 minutes. Drain the sweetbreads and discard the vegetables. Lay a piece of plastic wrap on a work surface. While the sweetbreads are still hot, place 2 at the bottom end of the plastic wrap. Roll the plastic around the sweetbreads tightly to form a cylinder. Twist the ends of the plastic to tighten and seal the package. Repeat with the other 2 sweetbreads. Refrigerate the packages until cool.

Meanwhile, bring a saucepan of lightly salted water to a boil over high heat. Have ready a bowl of ice water. Remove the stems from the Swiss chard and set aside. Add 4 nicely

continued ○ ○

shaped Swiss chard leaves to the boiling water and blanch until wilted, about 30 seconds. Using tongs or a slotted spoon, carefully transfer to the ice water to stop the cooking, taking care to keep the leaves whole. Keep the water at a boil. Drain the leaves, let cool, and transfer to paper towels to dry.

Cut the remaining Swiss chard leaves and stems into 1-inch julienne. Add to the boiling water and reduce the heat to medium. Cook until very tender, 5 to 8 minutes. Drain and shake well to dry. Transfer to a bowl and toss with 4 tablespoons of the olive oil. Season to taste with salt and pepper.

Place a whole blanched Swiss chard leaf in a 3-inch ring mold so that the leaf is flat in the bottom and hanging over the sides. Fill with one-fourth of the julienned chard and fold and tuck the leaf around the filling to make a nice circular bundle. Carefully remove from the ring and place the bundle, seam side down, on a baking sheet. Repeat with the remaining 3 leaves and julienned chard. Bake until heated through, 5 to 7 minutes.

Reheat the veal sauce and keep warm.

Brush the chops generously with olive oil and season with salt and pepper. Arrange on the grill and cook until medium-rare, 4 to 5 minutes on each side, or until an instant-read thermometer registers 120 degrees F when inserted into the thickest part. Be sure to get each side nicely browned and grill marked.

Remove the sweetbreads from the plastic wrap and cut into ½-inch slices. In a sauté pan, heat the remaining 2 tablespoons olive oil over medium-high heat. Add the sweetbreads and cook until crispy, about 2 minutes. Transfer to paper towels to drain.

To serve, place a Swiss chard timbale on the side of each of 4 warmed plates. Divide the sweetbread slices among the timbales, arranging them on top. Pool ¼ cup veal sauce on one side of each plate and set a veal chop on the sauce, with the bone end propped up on the timbale. Repeat to make the remaining 3 servings.

girello di vitello con polenta bianca

DOUBLE-ROASTED VEAL SHANK WITH WHITE CORN POLENTA

At Spiaggia, these falling-apart tender veal shanks are cooked twice: a long, slow braising and then a quick crisping in our wood-burning oven with high heat. You may not have a wood-burning oven, but a hot home oven produces spectacular results. This is a very popular dish at wine dinners, as the flavors go well with red wine. ○○ serves 4

½ cup extra-virgin olive oil

1 veal shank, about 4 pounds

Sea salt and freshly ground pepper

2 yellow onions, chopped

4 carrots, peeled and chopped

4 stalks celery, chopped

2 tablespoons tomato paste

5 sprigs fresh thyme

½ bunch fresh flat-leaf (Italian) parsley, stemmed and chopped

2 cups dry white wine

6 cups Veal Stock (page 33)

4 cups water

White Corn Polenta (page 42) for serving

4 sprigs fresh rosemary for garnish (optional)

Preheat the oven to 300 degrees F.

In a large, flameproof roasting pan or Dutch oven on top of the stove, heat the olive oil over medium-high heat. Season the shank with salt and pepper. Add to the pan and brown on all sides, 15 to 20 minutes. Transfer to a platter and set aside.

Add the onions, carrots, and celery to the roasting pan. Sauté until the vegetables are softened, about 5 minutes. Add the tomato paste, thyme, and parsley. Stir well to combine and cook until the vegetables are browned, 6 to 8 minutes longer. Add the wine and stir to scrape up any browned bits from the bottom of the pan.

Return the shank to the roasting pan with the vegetables. Add the stock and water. Cover the roasting pan with aluminum foil and bake until the shank pulls away from the bone, about 9 hours. Remove the shank and strain the liquid through a fine-mesh sieve into a saucepan, pressing on the solids with the back of a spoon. Discard the solids. Skim any excess fat from the braising liquid, bring to a simmer, and reduce until slightly thickened. Season the sauce to taste with salt and pepper. Keep warm.

Raise the oven temperature to 425 degrees F.

continued ○○

Place the veal upright in a lightly oiled nonstick roasting pan and roast until crispy, 25 to 30 minutes.

To serve, place ½ cup of polenta in the center of each of 4 warmed plates. Carve equal portions of the shank and place on top of the polenta. Ladle ¼ cup of the sauce on each plate. Garnish with rosemary sprigs and leaves, if using. Serve immediately.

note ○ ○ The veal shank can be presented whole and carved at the table.

agnello del colorado e spalle brasato d'agnello con purea di patate

GRILLED COLORADO LAMB CHOPS AND BRAISED LAMB SHOULDER
WITH POTATO PURÉE

Highlighting the meaty flavor of American lamb, this is one of Spiaggia's most sought-after recipes. The secret to this dish is the braised lamb shoulder. Do not use lamb shanks instead of the shoulder; the results will not be as good. The dual lamb preparations in this dish are indeed doubly satisfying—as if you're getting two meals for the price of one. ○○ serves 4

4 tablespoons extra-virgin olive oil, plus extra for brushing

2 cloves garlic, chopped, plus 8 whole cloves

1 small yellow onion, cut into chunks

2 carrots, peeled and cut into chunks

2 stalks celery, cut into chunks

2 bay leaves

2 pounds boneless lamb shoulder, cut into chunks

Sea salt and freshly ground pepper

6 fresh sprigs rosemary

1 cup Veal Sauce (page 39)

4 double-cut lamb rib chops

Basic Potato Purée (page 43) for serving

4 heads petit treviso, cleaned and trimmed, for garnish (optional)

In a large sauté pan or roasting pan over medium-high heat, heat 3 tablespoons of the olive oil. Add the chopped garlic and sauté until slightly browned, about 3 minutes. Add the onion, carrots, celery, and bay leaves and sauté until the vegetables start to caramelize, about 5 minutes. Season the shoulder meat with salt and pepper. Add to the pan and brown on both sides. Add enough water to cover the meat and scrape the bottom of the pan to loosen any browned bits. Add 2 of the rosemary sprigs. Bring to a boil, reduce the heat to low and cook gently, uncovered, until the meat has become falling-apart tender and most of the liquid has cooked down, 3 to 4 hours. Using tongs, transfer the meat from the liquid to a bowl and set aside to cool. Strain the braising liquid into another bowl and reserve. Discard the remaining solids.

Preheat the oven to 350 degrees F.

Put the 8 whole garlic cloves in a small saucepan with water to cover. Bring to a boil. Drain and repeat. Drain the cloves once more and set aside to dry.

Meanwhile, shred the braised lamb.

continued ○○

In a saucepan over medium-high heat, combine the veal sauce and 1 cup of the reserved braising liquid. Bring to a simmer, reduce the heat to medium, and cook to reduce by half, about 30 minutes. Set aside and keep warm.

In a saucepan, combine 2 cups of the braised lamb shoulder meat and ½ cup of the remaining reserved braising liquid and reheat gently. Keep warm.

Prepare the potato purée.

Prepare a fire in a charcoal grill or preheat a gas grill to 400 degrees F.

In a small sauté pan over medium heat warm the remaining 1 tablespoon olive oil. Add the whole garlic cloves and sauté until golden brown on all sides, about 4 minutes.

Brush the chops with olive oil and season with salt and pepper. Broil or grill the lamb until medium-rare, 3 to 4 minutes on each side, or until an instant-read thermometer registers 120 degrees F when inserted into the thickest part. Be sure to get each side nicely browned and grill marked.

To serve, place one-fourth of the shoulder meat in the center of each of 4 warmed plates. Place a grilled chop in front of the braised meat, with the bone pointing up. Spoon an oval of potato purée on the other side of the chop. Pour ¼ cup veal sauce over the chop and some on the plate. Repeat to make the remaining 3 servings. Garnish each with one of the remaining rosemary sprigs, 2 garlic cloves, and the petit treviso, if using. Serve immediately.

note ○○ Reserve any remaining braised lamb shoulder and/or liquid for another use.

costoletta di maiale senz'osso con polenta bianca e rapini

BONELESS PORK CHOP WITH WHITE CORN POLENTA
AND BROCCOLI RABE

Some pork producers are once again raising pork that isn't too lean; the resulting flavor reminds us of how good old-fashioned naturally raised pork can be. Be careful not to overcook the chops.

We love broccoli rabe and find it the perfect accompaniment to pork. Also known as *rapini,* it looks like broccoli but with longer stems and leaves and a slightly bitter taste. Broccoli rabe is best sautéed with garlic, with a sprinkling of red pepper flakes on top, if you like heat. When we shop on Harlem Avenue in the old Italian section of Chicago, we have to compete with the venerable Italian women even to get near the mountain of broccoli rabe at the main grocery store. In the produce section of our downtown grocer, there is plenty of room to pick out *rapini,* but it's not nearly as much fun. ○○ serves 4

4 cups water

¼ cup sugar

¼ cup salt

4 boneless pork loin chops, 5 ounces each

1 bunch broccoli rabe, about 1 pound (see Notes)

4 tablespoons extra-virgin olive oil, plus extra for drizzling

Freshly ground pepper

2 cups Chicken Stock (page 32) or prepared broth

1 large sprig fresh rosemary

2 tablespoons unsalted butter

Sea salt

1 clove garlic, thinly sliced

White Corn Polenta (page 42) for serving (see Notes)

In a large saucepan over medium heat, combine the water, sugar, and the ¼ cup salt. Heat the brine, stirring, until the sugar and salt dissolve. Let cool. Arrange the chops in a baking pan in a single layer and pour the cool brine over. Cover and refrigerate for 24 hours.

Preheat the oven to 425 degrees F.

Trim the broccoli rabe just below the leaves and discard the bottom inch of the stems. Have ready a bowl of ice water. Bring a saucepan of lightly salted water to a boil over high heat. Add the broccoli rabe and blanch for 1 minute.

Drain and plunge into the ice water to stop the cooking. Drain and chop into 1-inch pieces. Set aside.

continued ○○

Remove the chops from the brine and pat dry. In a large, ovenproof, nonstick sauté pan, heat 2 tablespoons of the olive oil over medium heat. Season the chops with pepper. When the pan and oil are hot, add the chops and cook for 5 minutes on one side. Turn them over, transfer to the oven, and bake until an instant-read thermometer registers 160 degrees F when inserted into the thickest part, 10 to 15 minutes. Transfer the chops to a platter, tent with aluminum foil, and keep warm.

Pour off any excess fat from the pan and place over medium-high heat. Add the stock and scrape any browned bits off the bottom of the pan. Add the rosemary, bring to a simmer, and cook until reduced by half, about 8 minutes. Remove from the heat, discard the rosemary, and whisk in the butter. Season to taste with salt and pepper. Set the sauce aside and keep warm.

In a sauté pan over medium-high heat, heat the remaining 2 tablespoons olive oil. Add the garlic and sauté until lightly browned. Add the blanched broccoli rabe and cook until crisp-tender, about 2 minutes. Season to taste with salt and pepper.

To serve, place ½ cup of the polenta in the center of each of 4 warmed plates. Slice a chop on the diagonal and arrange over the polenta. Arrange one-fourth of the broccoli rabe around the plate and drizzle with olive oil. Drizzle sauce around the polenta and on the plate in front of the meat. Repeat to make the remaining 3 servings. Serve immediately.

notes ○○ You can blanch and chop the broccoli rabe a day ahead and refrigerate it until needed. ○○ If you prefer, Basic Potato Purée (page 43) makes a perfect substitute for creamy polenta.

costolette di cinghiale con polenta taragna e pancetta

ROASTED BOAR CHOPS WITH BUCKWHEAT POLENTA AND BRAISED PORK BELLY

The boar is a very active animal; therefore, a little tenderizing from a daylong soak in brine is essential for juicy results from the grill. For an added dimension of flavor, the veal sauce served with this Umbrian farmhouse recipe includes fig *vin cotto,* a syrup made from dried grapes and figs. See Resources (page 186) for information on purchasing boar rib chops and *vin cotto.*
○ ○ serves 4

4 cups water	2 tablespoons olive oil for roasting
¼ cup salt	¼ cup extra-virgin olive oil
¼ cup sugar	2 cups Veal Sauce (page 39)
4 boar rib chops, frenched (cleaned bone; see recipe introduction)	¼ cup fig *vin cotto* (see recipe introduction) or *saba*
One 8-ounce piece fresh pork belly (see Notes)	Buckwheat Polenta (page 42) for serving

In a large saucepan over medium heat, combine the water, salt, and sugar. Heat the brine, stirring, until the sugar and salt dissolve. Let cool. Arrange the chops in a baking pan in a single layer and pour the cool brine over. Cover and refrigerate for 24 hours.

Preheat the oven to 275 degrees F. Place the pork belly in a heavy-bottomed ovenproof saucepan and sprinkle with olive oil. Roast until falling-apart tender, 6 to 8 hours. Remove from the oven and transfer to paper towels to drain. Cut into 4 equal squares and refrigerate until ready to use. Raise the oven temperature to 375 degrees F.

Remove the chops from the brine and pat dry. Heat the extra-virgin olive oil in a large ovenproof skillet over medium-high heat. Add the chops and sear for 2 to 3 minutes, turn, and transfer to the oven. Roast for 15 minutes for medium-rare, or until the desired doneness. Meanwhile, in a nonstick skillet, sear the squares of pork belly in the oven until crispy, about 5 minutes on each side. In a saucepan over medium heat, combine the veal sauce and *vin cotto* and heat until hot but not boiling. Set aside and keep warm.

On each of 4 warmed plates, spoon an oval of polenta on the left. Place a chop next to the polenta and a square of pork belly on the right. Ladle ½ cup of sauce in front of the chop.

notes ○ ○ Order fresh pork belly from the butcher two days before needed. ○ ○ Fresh figs and/or mâche lettuce (see page 49) are optional garnishes.

agnellino a latte al forno con patate

ROMAN-STYLE ROAST MILK-FED LAMB WITH CRISPY FINGERLING POTATOES

Slow roasting whole milk-fed lamb with lots of garlic and rosemary elevates the meat to something incredibly delicious and tender. Prepare this elegant feast for a large, festive gathering. ○○ serves 15 to 20

1 whole 25-pound milk-fed lamb, cleaned and dressed, cut into quarters by the butcher

Extra-virgin olive oil for rubbing

Sea salt and freshly ground pepper

Four 5-inch rosemary sprigs

5 heads garlic, cut in half

10 pounds fingerling potatoes, cut in half lengthwise

⅔ cup olive oil

Preheat the oven to 250 degrees F.

Rub the lamb with extra-virgin olive oil and season with salt and pepper. Place in a large nonstick or oiled roasting pan and roast until falling-off-the-bone tender, about 12 hours. For the last hour of cooking, add the rosemary and garlic.

One hour before serving, bring a large pot of lightly salted water to a boil. Add the potatoes and blanch them until slightly tender, but not cooked through. Drain well.

When the lamb is done, remove from the oven and set aside to rest. Increase the oven temperature to 450 degrees F. Add the ⅔ cup olive oil to a large roasting pan and heat in the oven for 5 minutes. Add the blanched potatoes and bake, turning every 10 minutes, until browned and crispy, yet moist on the inside, about 30 minutes. Transfer with a slotted spoon to paper towels to drain. Season the potatoes to taste with salt and pepper while they're still warm and transfer to a serving platter.

Place the lamb pieces on a large cutting board. As you carve, place a variety of cuts on each plate and serve with a spoonful of roasted potatoes.

I FORMAGGI italian cheeses

○ ○ ○ HISTORICALLY, EATING CHEESE AT THE END OF A MEAL WAS THOUGHT TO FACILITATE THE DIGESTION OF FOODS ALREADY CONSUMED. WHETHER OR NOT THIS IS TRUE, ENDING A MEAL WITH CHEESE IS A FINE WAY TO RELAX, FINISH THE WINE, AND CONTEMPLATE DESSERT.

CHEESE MAKING HAS LONG BEEN PART OF ITALIAN CULTURE. ALL GREAT CHEESE MAKERS RELY ON FINISHERS, OR *AFFINATORI*, TO COMPLETE THE PROCESS. THERE ARE SEVERAL *AFFINATORI* THROUGHOUT ITALY WITH REPUTATIONS OF TURNING OUT THE FINEST CHEESES, AND THEY IN TURN CATER TO THE BEST CHEESE PRODUCERS.

THE EUROPEAN CONCEPT OF FINISHING CHEESES IS AN ART THAT WE PRACTICE AT SPIAGGIA. WITH THE FIRST TEMPERATURE AND HUMIDITY-CONTROLLED CHEESE CAVE, AND THE FIRST FULL-TIME FORMAGGIAIO IN CHICAGO, WE TAKE CHEESE SERIOUSLY.

WE SERVE A SMALL SAMPLING OF CHEESES, TYPICALLY THREE TO FIVE SELECTIONS, TO COMPLEMENT AND ENHANCE THE DINING EXPERIENCE. WE HOPE THE GLEANINGS OF OUR EXPERIENCE THAT FOLLOW WILL HELP YOU WHEN PLANNING YOUR OWN CHEESE COURSE.

Make sure that the cheese you purchase is in peak condition. Insist that your purveyor let you sample the cheese. Smell it. If it has an off aroma, reject it. Look at it. If it is discolored near the rind, it is likely too old and its flavor is declining. Feel it. Very few cheeses are slimy by nature, so if it is, reject it. And lastly, taste it. Is the flavor what you were expecting? Is it bright and clean and explosive in the mouth? Would it satisfy you if you were a guest? If so, buy it, but have the purveyor cut a piece from the wheel. Many cheeses decline in flavor if separated from the wheel for long, which is why you should buy all of your cheese as closely as possible to the time you plan to use it, preferably the same day. Also remember to take the cheese out of the refrigerator at least 30 minutes before serving, so that it can breathe and warm up. Cheese is nearly twice as flavorful if consumed at room temperature.

When selecting which varieties you will serve, seek balance in every aspect: milk, flavor, texture, and intensity. Try to have at least one cheese that is strong, one that is mild, and one that is in-between. The textures should vary from hard to rich and creamy. The texture is largely controlled by age: the longer your cheese is aged, the harder it will be. Soft cheeses are usually aged for up to 8 weeks, while a medium-textured cheese is usually aged longer. Blue-veined cheeses need at least 3 months of aging, but can be quite creamy. Hard-textured cheeses are typically aged for at least 6 months and up to several years. Also, offer one cheese of each type of milk: goat, typically very sharp and nutty; sheep, usually earthy and pungent; and cow, the flavor and strength of which vary considerably and depend on the cheese-making technique. A cow's milk cheese can be found to match the taste of any guest.

The best and most famous Italian hard cheese is Parmigiano-Reggiano. Made from cow's milk, it has a fine, crumbly texture and sweet, cleansing flavor. It is aged for at least 14 months, but most Parmigiano-Reggiano on the market has been aged for at least 2 years. American-made Parmesan cheeses cannot match the unique, complex flavor and texture of true Parmigiano-Reggiano. Widely known as a grating cheese, Parmigiano-Reggiano also dazzles the taste buds when eaten on its own.

The widest varieties of Italian cheeses available in America are made from goat's or sheep's milk. Sheep's milk cheeses go by the name pecorino, and range from the truffle-infused pecorino tartufato to the dry, sharp, and somewhat briny pecorino romano. Most Italian goat's milk cheeses are known by the name caprino. Typically young and sweet, they can be flavored in numerous ways, from an infusion of truffles to Barolo wine. Italy also produces a number of blue-veined cheeses. Though varying, they tend to have one thing in common—they are all powerhouses. They can range from sweet to sharp, as with Gorgonzola *dolce* or *normale,* but they always pack a big flavor.

During the past twenty-five years, American dairy farmers and cheese makers have been producing artisanal cheeses based on Italian and French styles. We include a variety of these American cheeses on our cheese menu at Spiaggia.

Remember, too, for every cheese there is a wine, and for every wine a cheese.

nocciole caramellate

CANDIED NUTS

In America, it's common to pair cheese with contrasting flavors. These sweet nuts go well with the natural saltiness of goat cheese. ○○ makes 2 cups

2 cups whole nuts, such as walnuts and/or hazelnuts (see Notes), cashews, or almonds, or a mixture

¾ cup sugar

¼ cup water

Preheat the oven to 350 degrees F. Oil a large baking sheet.

Spread the nuts in a single layer on a separate baking sheet and toast until a very light brown, 5 to 10 minutes. Transfer immediately to a plate to cool.

Combine the sugar and water in a saucepan, and stir to dissolve the sugar. Bring to a boil over high heat. Continue to boil, brushing down the pan sides with water to prevent crystals from forming, until the water is reduced and the syrup starts to color. Reduce the heat to medium and continue to cook the caramel until it is a light, even brown, stirring constantly. Add the nuts all at once and stir them in. The sugar will seize up at first because the nuts cool it off. Continue cooking and stirring to loosen the mixture. When it starts to get fluid again, keep a very close eye on it. As soon as either the nuts or the caramel darkens more, remove from the heat and pour the mixture onto the prepared baking sheet. Use a wooden spoon to spread the mixture out evenly and quickly, separating the nuts as much as possible before the caramel hardens.

notes ○○ If using hazelnuts, remove the skins after toasting by rubbing the warm nuts vigorously in a clean cloth. ○○ Candied Nuts can be stored in an airtight container, away from heat and light, for up to 1 week.

mostarda fatta in casa di arancia e limone

SPIAGGIA'S ORANGE AND LEMON MOSTARDA

This is our recipe for the tangy, sweet-spicy condiment Italians use in confections and serve with boiled meats and cheese. ○○ **makes 1 cup**

4 oranges or lemons or a mixture of both	2 cups sugar
3 cups water	1½ tablespoons mustard oil

Zest the oranges and lemons in thin strips. Reserve the fruit for another use.

Put the zest in a large saucepan and cover with cold water. Bring to a simmer over medium heat and cook for 2 minutes. Drain and repeat 2 more times.

Return the zest to the pan and add the water and sugar. Raise the heat to medium-high and cook, stirring, for about 2 minutes. Reduce the heat to a low simmer and cook until the zest begins to become translucent, 15 to 20 minutes.

Remove from the heat and, with a slotted spoon, transfer the zest to a bowl. Add the mustard oil to the zest, stirring well to combine. Pour the mixture onto a shallow pan, spreading it out in a thin layer to cool. Top with just enough of the syrup to cover. Reserve any leftover syrup for another use.

Let cool, transfer to an airtight container, and refrigerate until ready to use.

notes ○○ Save the leftover syrup for your next batch. ○○ *Mostarda* can be refrigerated, in an airtight container, for up to 2 months.

I DOLCI desserts

○ ○ ○ AT SPIAGGIA, DESSERTS ARE ABOUT AUTHENTIC FLAVORS AND AUTHENTIC INGREDIENTS USED CREATIVELY, WITHOUT COMPROMISING QUALITY.

MASCARPONE CHEESE, HAZELNUTS, MOSCATO, ESPRESSO, AND AMARETTO ARE JUST SOME OF THE TRADITIONAL INGREDIENTS WE USE TO COMPOSE OUR DESSERTS. (YES, WE USE EGGS, BUTTER, AND SUGAR, TOO.)

WE LIKE TO SAY THAT THE PERFECT ENDING TO A GREAT ITALIAN MEAL OCCURS AT THE END OF DESSERT—WHEN THE ESPRESSO IS SERVED. TRULY, DESSERT ISN'T OVER UNTIL YOU'VE HAD YOUR ESPRESSO. AT SPIAGGIA, WE SERVE ONLY ONE BRAND OF ESPRESSO, ILLY. ONE SIP OF THIS COFFEE VIRTUALLY TRANSPORTS YOU TO ITALY. ILLY ESPRESSO ALSO TASTES GREAT IN OUR ESPRESSO SAUCE (SEE PAGE 170).

sformato di moscato d'asti ai frutti di bosco

DESSERT WINE GELATIN WITH FRESH BERRIES

This dessert is delicious because of its simple, clean flavors. Moscato is a sweet, sparkling Italian wine that is both fruity and refreshing. Quick and easy to prepare, this sweet treat is at its best when the berries are at their peak. ○○ serves 8

2 cups Moscato d'Asti wine or sparkling white grape juice

⅔ cup sugar

2 envelopes unflavored gelatin (2 tablespoons)

1½ cups fresh raspberries

1⅓ cups fresh blueberries

Whipped Cream (page 45) or fresh berries for garnish (optional)

In a small saucepan, heat ½ cup of the wine over medium heat until hot but not boiling. Pour the hot wine into a large nonaluminum bowl and immediately stir in the sugar. Allow the mixture to stand for 2 to 3 minutes. Pour the gelatin into a small bowl and stir in the remaining 1½ cups of wine. When the gelatin has dissolved, add this mixture to the sweetened wine and stir well to blend.

In a small bowl, gently toss the berries together and fill eight 4-ounce individual cups or molds two-thirds full of fruit. Spoon ¼ cup gelatin mixture over the fruit in each cup. Refrigerate until the gelatin has set and is firm to the touch, 2 to 3 hours.

To unmold, dip the bottom of each cup or mold in very hot water for 5 seconds and invert immediately onto a dessert plate. Garnish each serving with whipped cream or additional berries, if using.

torta al mascarpone in salsa di illy caffè

MASCARPONE TORTE WITH ILLY ESPRESSO SAUCE

Mascarpone is a fresh cow's-milk cheese from northern Italy. Creamy and rich, mascarpone, in the guise of tiramisù, has conquered America. Our elegant rendition of tiramisù highlights the slight tang and voluptuous texture of the imported cheese. ○○ serves 8

1¼ cups sugar

6 egg yolks

2 envelopes unflavored gelatin (2 tablespoons)

2¼ pounds mascarpone cheese

2 cups Whipped Cream (see page 45)

8 very thin slices pound cake

¼ cup brewed espresso coffee, cooled

1 tablespoon coffee liqueur such as Kahlúa

½ cup unsweetened cocoa powder

8 fresh mint leaves

1 pint fresh raspberries

In a large bowl set over (but not touching) a pan of barely simmering water, whisk together the sugar and egg yolks. When warm, add the gelatin. Whisk the mixture until pale in color, about 5 minutes. Remove from the heat.

Using an electric mixer, whip the mixture on high speed for 3 minutes. Add the mascarpone cheese and whip until well combined, about 2 minutes longer. Fold in the cream. Reserve 2½ cups of the mascarpone mixture for the espresso sauce.

Divide the remainder of the mixture among eight 4-inch individual molds (there may be a small amount left over). Cut out a 3-inch round from each pound cake slice. Place a cake round on top of each mold. (This will prevent the dessert from sliding when served.) Freeze overnight.

To unmold, dip the bottom of each mold in very hot water halfway up the sides for 5 seconds and invert immediately onto a plate. Refrigerate for 1 hour before serving.

In a large bowl, stir together the espresso and liqueur. Fold into the reserved mascarpone mixture and mix until well combined. If it seems too thick, add a little heavy cream.

To serve, pool ¼ cup of sauce in the center of each of 8 chilled plates. Using a spatula, carefully pick up 1 torte and, over a separate plate, dust the top with cocoa powder. Place the torte on top of the espresso sauce and garnish the plate with a mint leaf and a few raspberries. Repeat to make the remaining 7 servings.

tartalette di cioccolato amaro in salsa di mandorle tostate

BITTERSWEET CHOCOLATE TARTLETS WITH TOASTED ALMOND SAUCE

These individual tarts are not only sinfully delicious, they are also very pretty. The almond sauce is a versatile topping; try it with any favorite chocolate, caramel, or coffee-flavored dessert. ○○ serves 8

For the Sweet Pastry:

1¼ cups cake flour

⅓ cup sugar

½ cup plus 2 tablespoons cold unsalted butter, cut into small pieces

2 egg yolks, lightly beaten

2 tablespoons ice water

For the Filling:

¾ cup heavy cream

⅓ cup whole milk

7½ ounces bittersweet chocolate, preferably Valrhona, coarsely chopped

1 egg

For the Almond Sauce:

1⅓ cups slivered almonds

1 cup sugar

4 cups whole milk

8 egg yolks

Whipped Cream (page 45) for garnish (optional)

To make the pastry: In a bowl, whisk together the flour and sugar. Add the butter and cut into the dry ingredients using a fork, 2 knives, or a pastry blender. When the butter pieces are well blended with the dry ingredients and no larger than small peas, turn the dough out onto a lightly floured work surface. Make a well in the center, add the egg yolks and water, and use a fork to gradually combine the liquids with the flour mixture. When combined, knead the dough until it forms a smooth ball, 2 to 3 minutes. Cover the dough with plastic and refrigerate for 30 minutes.

Have ready eight 4-inch nonstick tartlet pans. If you don't have nonstick pans, grease the pans and dust with flour.

continued ○○

Remove the dough from the refrigerator and let warm for 2 to 3 minutes before rolling.

Work on a cool surface, away from the oven. Flour the work surface and the dough to avoid sticking. Flatten the dough and roll out from the middle. When the dough is about ⅛ inch thick, cut it into eight 5-inch rounds. Using your fingers, press each dough round gently into the bottom and sides of a tartlet pan. Prick the dough with a fork and refrigerate for 30 minutes before baking.

Preheat the oven to 400 degrees F. Arrange the tartlet pans on a baking sheet and place pie weights or dried beans in each pan to keep the dough from rising as it bakes. Bake until the pastry is golden brown, 10 to 15 minutes. Transfer the pans to wire racks to cool. Reduce the oven temperature to 375 degrees F.

To make the filling: In a saucepan over medium heat, combine the cream and milk and bring to a simmer. Add the chocolate and whisk until melted. Remove from the heat and whisk in the egg until well blended, about 2 minutes.

Return the tartlet shells to the baking sheet and pour in the filling, dividing it evenly. Return to the oven and bake until the centers are set, 15 to 18 minutes. Remove from the oven and let cool.

Meanwhile, make the almond sauce: Have ready a large bowl of ice water. In a saucepan over low heat, combine the almonds with ½ cup of the sugar. Toast slowly, stirring often, until the almonds have browned and the sugar is caramelized, about 8 minutes. Add the milk and whisk until well combined. Slowly bring the mixture to a boil. Remove from the heat and strain through a fine-mesh sieve. Discard the almonds. Return the liquid to the saucepan and keep warm over low heat.

In a metal bowl set over (but not touching) a pan of simmering water, whisk together the egg yolks and the remaining ½ cup sugar until thick and pale, about 2 minutes. Gradually add half of the hot milk mixture to the egg-yolk mixture and whisk vigorously to combine. Add the egg-yolk mixture to the pan with the remaining milk mixture. Place over medium-low heat and continue whisking until the custard has thickened and comes to a boil. Remove from the heat and stir for 1 minute. Place the pan in the bowl of ice water and stir to cool.

To serve, place the tartlets on individual plates and ladle ¼ cup of the almond sauce around each tartlet. Garnish each serving with whipped cream, if using.

focaccia alle noci con crema di vaniglia e frutti di bosco all'aceto balsamico

ALMOND AND HAZELNUT FOCACCIA CAKE WITH VANILLA CREAM AND BALSAMIC-MARINATED BERRIES

Our friend and colleague Massimo Ferrari hails from the Mantova area. He refers to this cake as "dessert focaccia." This "focaccia" bakes up like a cookie but is transformed into a cake when layered with vanilla cream. It should be made 1 day before you plan on serving it, to allow the flavors to deepen. Hazelnut and almond flours can be found at natural foods stores and well-stocked supermarkets. ○○ serves 8

For the Vanilla Cream:

1 cup whole milk

2 egg yolks

5 tablespoons granulated sugar

⅛ cup unbleached all-purpose flour

½ teaspoon vanilla extract

For the Cake:

½ cup hazelnut flour

½ cup almond flour

2 cups unbleached all-purpose flour

1¼ cups confectioners' sugar

1 cup unsalted butter, at room temperature

½ teaspoon vanilla extract

½ cup fresh strawberries, quartered

½ cup fresh raspberries

½ cup fresh blackberries

½ cup fresh blueberries

2 tablespoons Balsamic Reduction (page 36)

Confectioners' sugar for dusting (optional)

To make the vanilla cream: Have ready a bowl of ice water. In a saucepan over medium-high heat, bring the milk to a boil. Reduce the heat to low to keep warm.

In a metal bowl set over (but not touching) a pan of simmering water, whisk together the egg yolks, granulated sugar, and flour until thick and pale, about 2 minutes. Gradually add half of the hot milk to the egg-yolk mixture, whisking vigorously to combine.

Return the egg-yolk mixture to the saucepan with the remaining hot milk. Place over medium-low heat and continue whisking until the custard has thickened and comes to

continued ○○

a boil. Remove from the heat, add the vanilla, and continue to stir for a few seconds to keep the mixture from overcooking. Place the pan in the bowl of ice water and let cool. When cool, pour the vanilla cream onto a platter. Using a rubber spatula, spread the cream out evenly and smooth the top. Cover with plastic wrap and refrigerate until chilled.

To make the cake: Preheat the oven to 350 degrees F. Lightly grease a baking sheet and line with parchment paper.

In a bowl, whisk together the flours and confectioners' sugar and set aside.

In a stand mixer using the paddle attachment, beat the butter on high speed until pale and fluffy, 5 to 6 minutes. Reduce the speed to low and beat in the vanilla. Add the dry ingredients to the butter mixture and beat until a soft dough forms.

Turn the dough out onto a lightly floured work surface. Divide the dough in half and shape each into a disk. Roll out each disk into a round about 8 inches in diameter and ¼ inch thick. Transfer to the prepared baking sheet and bake until golden on top and lightly browned on the bottom, 20 to 25 minutes. Transfer to wire racks to cool completely.

When cool, transfer 1 cake layer to a large plate. Spread with a thin layer of vanilla cream and place the second cake layer on top. Transfer to an airtight container or wrap well in plastic and refrigerate overnight.

When ready to serve, in a bowl, gently combine all the berries with the balsamic reduction. Let stand at room temperature for 5 minutes to allow the flavors to meld.

To serve, cut the cake into 8 wedges. Place each piece on a chilled plate and top with ¼ cup of the marinated berries. Dust with a little confectioners' sugar, if using, and serve.

note ○○ Gelato can be used as a substitute for the marinated berries (as pictured).

macedonia ai frutti di bosco con gelato alla menta

WARM BERRY SOUP WITH MINT GELATO

This soup warms both body and soul, and is easy and quick to prepare. You can substitute purchased mint gelato or ice cream for the homemade. ○○ serves 8

For the Mint Gelato:

3 cups whole milk

1 cup half-and-half

1¼ cups sugar

1½ cups loosely packed fresh mint leaves, chopped

1 cup liquid pasteurized egg yolks (8 egg yolks)

2 teaspoons green crème de menthe

2 tablespoons unsalted butter

4 tablespoons sugar

4 cups mixed fresh berries, such as strawberries, blueberries, raspberries, and blackberries

Juice of 2 lemons

3 cups water

1 cup Raspberry Sauce (page 45)

Leaves from 8 sprigs fresh mint for garnish

To make the gelato: In a saucepan, combine the milk, half-and-half, ¾ cup of the sugar, and the chopped mint and bring to a boil. Remove from the heat, strain through a fine-mesh sieve, and return to the saucepan. Keep warm over low heat. Discard the mint.

In a bowl, whisk together the remaining ½ cup sugar and the egg yolks until combined, about 2 minutes. Gradually add half of the hot milk mixture to the egg-yolk mixture and whisk vigorously to combine. Return the egg-yolk mixture to the pan with the remaining milk mixture. Return to medium heat and stir constantly with a wooden spoon until thick enough to coat the back of the spoon, 4 to 6 minutes. Do not let it boil; overheating will break the custard. Remove from the heat and continue to stir for a few seconds to keep the mixture from overcooking. Stir in the crème de menthe. Let cool, cover, and refrigerate until well chilled, at least 3 hours or preferably overnight.

Pour the custard into an ice-cream maker and freeze following the manufacturer's instructions. Transfer to a freezer-safe container and freeze until firm, at least 3 hours.

In a large saucepan over medium heat, melt the butter. Add the sugar and whisk to combine. Add the berries and sauté for 2 minutes. Add the lemon juice, water, and raspberry sauce and bring to a simmer over low heat.

Remove from the heat and ladle into 8 warmed bowls. Top each serving with a scoop of the gelato and garnish with mint leaves. Serve immediately.

note o o You can prepare this recipe to serve 4, by halving the ingredient measures for the berry soup. Make the gelato as directed on page 178 and serve generous portions.

bomboloni con zabaglione alla grappa di moscato

HANDMADE DONUTS WITH GRAPPA DI MOSCATO ZABAGLIONE

Dipped in a grappa zabaglione, these warm, sugary delights are creamy and crispy at the same time. Grappa is a clear, strong liquor distilled from grapes. It is usually named for the grape from which it was distilled. We like to use *grappa di Moscato* for this recipe because the alcohol cuts through the richness of the sauce and the Moscato flavor sweetens without being too sweet. We make these in large batches and savor the leftovers! ○○ serves 10 to 14

For the Bomboloni:

One 2-ounce cake fresh yeast or 3 packages active dry yeast

¼ cup warm water

½ cup sugar

1 egg

2 tablespoons unsalted butter, melted

½ cup whole milk

½ teaspoon salt

4 cups unbleached all-purpose flour

For the Zabaglione:

7 egg yolks

½ cup sugar

Pinch of salt

½ cup water

¼ cup *grappa di Moscato*

1 cup heavy cream, whipped to soft peaks

1 cup sugar for coating

Canola oil for deep-frying

To make the bombolini: In a bowl, whisk together the yeast, water, and ¼ cup of the sugar. Let stand for about 10 minutes so that the yeast can bloom. When the yeast is foamy, transfer to the bowl of a stand mixer fitted with the dough hook attachment. Mix in the egg, butter, milk, salt, and the remaining ¼ cup sugar. Slowly add in the flour and mix until smooth.

Transfer the dough to a lightly greased bowl and cover with plastic wrap. Let the dough rise in a warm place until doubled in bulk, about 1 hour.

Punch down the dough, turn out onto a lightly floured work surface, and roll out about ¼ inch thick. Use a 1-inch round cookie cutter to cut out as many rounds as possible from

continued ○○

the dough, using all the dough. (Do not combine and reuse scraps.) Place on floured baking sheets and let rise until doubled again, about 10 minutes.

Meanwhile, make the zabaglione: Have ready a large bowl of ice water. In a metal bowl set over (but not touching) a pan of simmering water, whisk together the egg yolks, ½ cup sugar, salt, water, and grappa until thick and pale, about 10 minutes. Remove from the heat, place the pan in the bowl of ice water, and stir to cool. When cool, fold in the whipped cream. Set aside.

Put the 1 cup sugar in a shallow dish and set aside. In a large, heavy-bottomed pot over high heat, pour in oil to a depth of 8 inches. Heat to 350 degrees F on a deep-frying thermometer. Add one-third of the *bomboloni* and fry, turning once, until golden, 30–60 seconds per side. Transfer to paper towels to drain. While still warm, toss in a little sugar to coat. Repeat with the remaining batches.

Serve the *bomboloni* warm, with the zabaglione.

acknowledgments

SPIAGGIA AND THIS COOKBOOK WOULD NOT EXIST WITHOUT THE VISION AND SUPPORT OF LARRY LEVY. HIS ENTHUSIASM FOR ALL THINGS SPIAGGIA IS UNPARALLELED.

It is a privilege to thank these fine people for their hard work and dedication in making The Spiaggia Cookbook a reality.

Our great staff at Spiaggia, for showing up each and every day, and making it all happen. Christine Tully and Aniel Chopra, for taking charge of the cookbook project and keeping us all communicating and focused; Gianni Toffanello, for his *voce italiano;* Henry Bishop III, *"il sommelier più pazzo del mondo"*; and Karima Bentounsi for her expert typing and organizational skills.

Our tireless team of professionals in the kitchen, Missy Robbins, Beth Partridge, Efrain Medrano, Michael Griggs, Richard Camarota, Lupe Tiscareno, Michael Farrel, and Dan Pancake for their talents at the stove and the culinary passion in their hearts.

Jeff Kauck, for his beautiful photography of Spiaggia's food, styled by Will Smith.

Leslie Jonath, Pamela Geismar, Jane Chinn, Laurel Mainard, Jan Hughes, and the staff at Chronicle Books, for their patient guidance in shaping our manuscript, and Lisa Billard and Hallie Overman of Lisa Billard Design for their fantastic layout.

Andy Lansing, Mary Wagstaff, Janet Isabelli, Alison Weber, Gina Johnson, Michael Perlberg, Kirsten Mentley, and Claudia Sutherland, for their expertise in their provinces of executive direction, public relations, law, creative direction, and recipe testing.

Our friends in Italy, who in 1983 opened their kitchens and their hearts to two young Americans: *grazie mille* to Eugenio Medagliani, Antonio and Nadia Santini, Romano and Franca Franceschini, Sauro Brunacardi, Massimo and Maria Ferrari, Roberto Ferrari, and the late Franco Colombani.

Sue Piette, our first proofreader, and Donna Alden, the best at-home cook and accidental recipe tester we know.

All of our guests who have visited Spiaggia during the last twenty years, especially those who have become our friends, we appreciate their support.

The farmers, anglers, artisans, and purveyors who diligently supply Spiaggia with the best and sometimes-hard-to-find foodstuffs that we serve each day. We especially cheer those who locally work long hours, wearing all the hats of small business, bringing us incredible, fresh, homegrown products.

Bernardaud and Material Possessions for their artful tablewares.

Those who have inspired us the most: We are forever indebted to Gisella and Sam Mantuano, Dorothy and Eugene Mantuano, Filomena and Michele Pietrangelo, and Rose and John Roeske. And to Carlo Mantuano, thanks for eating dozens of restaurant meals from Piemonte to Calabria, and all the regions in between, for putting up with the late nights at work, and for tasting all the dishes in this book.

resources

BOTTEGA DEL VINO
Gorgeous, hand-blown glassware from Italy.
775 West Jackson Boulevard,
Chicago, IL 60661 ○○ 888.Del.Vino

BROWNE TRADING
High-quality fish, such as red mullet and
salt cod, and shellfish of all kinds, including
langoustinos and red shrimp.
260 Commercial Street, No .3,
Portland, ME 04101 ○○ 800.944.7848
○○ www.browne-trading.com

D'ARTAGNAN
Boar chops, duck foie gras, truffles, truffle
oil, game birds and game meats.
280 Wilson Avenue, Newark, NJ 07105
973.344.0565 ○○ www.dartagnan.com

EARTHY DELIGHTS
A great selection of oils, vinegars, and
hard-to-find gourmet produce.
1161 East Clark Road, Suite 260,
DeWitt, MI 48820 ○○ 800.367.4709
○○ www.earthy.com

**GREAT AMERICAN CHEESE
COLLECTION**
The finest in artisanal domestic cheeses.
2320 West 110th Street, Chicago,
IL 60643 ○○ 773.779.5055
○○ www.greatamericancheese.com

ILLYCAFFÈ NORTH AMERICA, INC.
Espresso coffee.
200 Clearbrook Road, Elmsford, NY
10523 ○○ 800.USA.ILLY
○○ www.illyusa.com

ISOLA IMPORTS
Vin cotto and other imported products.
1321 Grand Avenue, Chicago, IL 60622
773.342.2121○ ○www.isolaimports.com

L'ALBERGHIERA MEDAGLIANI
Brass *torchio* (*bigolaro*) extrusion
machines and other utensils and cookware.
via S.Gregorio 43, 20125 Milano, Italy
t:+39.02.66983073 / f:+39.02.6701113
○○ www.medagliani.com

MEATS BY LINZ
Specialists in gourmet restaurant-quality
beef, veal, pork, and lamb.
439 Burnham Avenue, Calumet City, IL
60409 ○○ 708.862.0830
○○ www.meatsbylinz.com

MOZZARELLA COMPANY
Fresh mozzarella by Paula Lambert as
well as many other impeccable handcrafted
cheeses including Crescenza cheese.
2944 Elm Street, Dallas, TX 75226
214.741.4071
○○ www.mozzarellacompany.com

PRAIRIE GROVE FARMS
One hundred percent natural pork, raised
free of antibiotics and hormones.
125 North First Street, DeKalb, IL
60115 ○○ 815.754.0880
○○ www.prairiegrovefarms.com

SID WAINER & SON
Pantry items such as truffles, smoked
seafood, fresh fruits, and hard-to-find vegetables such as cardoons and fava beans.
2301 Purchase Street, New Bedford,
MA 02746 ○○ 800.423.8333
○○ www.sidwainer.com

SUR LA TABLE
Cookware, utensils, appliances, and the
chitarra pasta machine.
1765 Sixth Avenue South, Seattle, WA
98134 ○○ 866.328.5412 and
800.243.0852 ○○ www.surlatable.com

TEKLA, INC.
Importer Sofia Solomon carries only the
best in caviar, fish roe, agrumato oil, cheese,
legumes (Peruvian lima beans), and chocolate.
1456 North Dayton Street, Chicago, IL
60622 ○○ 312.915.5914

THE CHEF'S GARDEN, INC.
The Jones family grows and picks the
finest gourmet vegetables, fruits, herbs,
lettuces, edible flowers, heirloom tomatoes,
and microgreens.
9009 Huron-Avery Road, Huron, OH
44839 ○○ 800.289.4644
○○ www.chefs-garden.com

URBANI TRUFFLES USA, LTD.
Top quality truffles and truffle paste.
380 Meadowbrook Road, North Wales,
PA 19454 ○○ 215.699.8780
○○ www.urbanitruffles.com

WILLIAMS-SONOMA
Pasta, salts, olive oils, and many pantry items
as well as olive oil and vinegar tasting bars
in its retail stores.
3250 Van Ness Avenue, San Francisco,
CA 94109 ○○ 877.812.6235
○○ www.williams-sonoma.com

VIOLA IMPORTS INC.
Italian specialty products
P.O. Box 185 Elk Grove Village, IL
60009 ○○ www.voilaimports.com

index

table of equivalents

The exact equivalents in the following tables have been rounded for convenience.

Liquid/Dry Measures

u.s.	metric	u.s.	metric
¼ teaspoon	1.25 milliliters	1 cup	240 milliliters
½ teaspoon	2.5 milliliters	1 pint (2 cups)	480 milliliters
1 teaspoon	5 milliliters	1 quart (4 cups, 32 ounces)	960 milliliters
1 tablespoon (3 teaspoons)	15 milliliters	1 gallon (4 quarts)	3.84 liters
1 fluid ounce (2 tablespoons)	30 milliliters	1 ounce (by weight)	28 grams
¼ cup	60 milliliters	1 pound	454 grams
⅓ cup	80 milliliters	2.2 pounds	1 kilogram
½ cup	120 milliliters		

Length

u.s.	metric
⅛ inch	3 millimeters
¼ inch	6 millimeters
½ inch	12 millimeters
1 inch	2.5 centimeters

Oven Temperature

fahrenheit	celsius	gas	fahrenheit	celsius	gas
250	120	½	400	200	6
275	140	1	425	220	7
300	150	2	450	230	8
325	160	3	475	240	9
350	180	4	500	260	10
375	190	5